LET
CHRIST
BE KING

LET CHRIST BE KING

REFLECTIONS ON THE LIFE AND TIMES OF ABRAHAM KUYPER

L. PRAAMSMA

PAIDEIA PRESS
Jordan Station, Ontario, Canada

Canadian Cataloguing in Publication Data

Praamsma, L. (Louis), 1910–1984
    Let Christ be king

ISBN 0-88815-064-4

1. Kuyper, Abraham, 1837–1920.   2. Statesmen –
Netherlands – Biography.   3. Theologians –
Netherlands – Biography.   4. Netherlands –
History – 1849–   I. Title.

DJ283.K89P72   1985   949.2'06'0924   C85-098063-1

Cover design by Gerrit V.L. Verstraete, Christian Communications Centre,
Toronto.

ISBN 0-88815-064-4
Printed in Canada.

Contents

Chapter 1

The Spirit of the Nineteenth Century

The idea of the spirit of a time

Emile Durkheim (1858-1917), the founder of modern sociology, was convinced that a society has a "collective consciousness," which consists of the feelings and beliefs shared by the "average men," by the majority.[1] He was not the first to propose that a society directs and is directed, that it acts and reacts, and that it is marked by a certain kind of spirit. A century before Durkheim, J.G. von Herder (1744-1803) had launched similar ideas in his book *Ideas for the Philosophy of the History of Mankind.*

Herder, who was one of the first representatives of Romanticism, spoke of the *Geist* (spirit) of humanity, which comes to ever fuller expression in consecutive stages. He influenced the Groningen theology of The Netherlands in the first half of the nineteenth century. This theology, in turn, influenced the young Abraham Kuyper.

It should not surprise us, then, that in Kuyper's works we find many a reference to the "spirit of the time" or, as Isaac Da Costa, a poet greatly admired by Kuyper, put it, the "spirit of the age."* However, unlike Herder, who expected to witness the dawning of an age of true humanity, Kuyper detected dangerous tendencies toward deterioration and godlessness in the "spirit of the time."

He once pointed to the remarkable fact that we sometimes find a certain heresy knocking at the door of the church in

---

* In 1823 Da Costa had published his "Objections against the spirit of the age."

7

several places at the same time, yet without any apparent collusion. He commented: "We speak of the spirit of an age, and anyone who compares the spirit of the age of the Reformation with that of the age of the French Revolution, or the spirit of the eighteenth century with that of the nineteenth century, immediately feels that there is an essential difference between the one age and the other." He wrote about various aspects and factors which express the spirit of a time, such as public opinion, the style and fashion of life, and the general way of thinking and speaking. Yet not even all its facets and expressions can sufficiently explain the dynamics of the spirit of the time. Hence Kuyper wrote: "Behind and in those demonstrable factors there is also a common moving power (*drijfkracht*) which escapes our analysis and is caused by mysterious influences from the spiritual world." He then cited the words of the apostle Paul: "We are not contending against flesh and blood, but against the principalities, against the powers, against the world rulers of this present darkness, against the spiritual hosts of wickedness in the heavenly places" (Eph. 6:12).[2]

This is a sound historical assessment. History does indeed occur in periods. Although it is sometimes rather difficult to find the starting point of a certain era and although there are some long, drawn-out transitional periods, it is an undeniable fact that each special time has its own special face. That face is marked by several features: some of them have a genealogy, but not all of them. There are old elements and new ones; there is continuity and discontinuity in every civilization. We find the ever-abiding work of the Holy Spirit in the Church of Jesus Christ, but we also find the actions and reactions, the inventions and distortions, the obedience and disobedience of the spirit of man. Moreover, we find mysterious and hidden impulses, irrational and sometimes overwhelming passions, which point to the one who is called the "murderer from the beginning" (John 8:44).

History never repeats itself. Although we recognize historical parallels, and although no human power can change the human condition, so that even the Bible tells us that there is nothing new under the sun (Eccl. 1:9), we never walk in circles. As age succeeds age, we live in an ever more complex and riper world.

We want to get to know Abraham Kuyper in the context of his own time. What was the special character of his time? What was the spirit of the age?

There is a definite starting point to be found: Kuyper, like his predecessor, Groen van Prinsterer, always referred to a certain point of departure in characterizing his own time—the formidable events of the French Revolution of 1789. In their view, this revolution was the consummation and zenith, but at the same time the downfall and destruction, of the hopes and ideals of the eighteenth century.

The revolution was the culmination of the rationalism, deism, naturalism, and materialism of the period that preceded it. It was also a judgment upon the abuses of that period, which had become evident in tyranny, antiquated feudalism, and the cries of the suppressed lower classes. In Robespierres's reign of terror and in Napoleon's reign of the gun, the revolution also turned into a caricature of its own high ideals of freedom, equality and fraternity.

The nineteenth century was in the first place a reaction against the frightening aspects of the French Revolution. Yet at the same time it carried the ideas of the French Revolution further. It opened the door both to reaction and to liberalism, to conservatism and to socialism, to all manner of new theologies and to a revival of the old one, to secularism and evangelism, and to agnostic idealism. It was a time of many great names—the time of Schleiermacher and Hegel, of Darwin and Marx, of Bismarck and Gladstone, of Newman and Kierkegaard.

Among these great names, the name of Abraham Kuyper deserves to be mentioned. When he was young he assimilated all the new ideas of his time. However, when it pleased God to convert him, he used all the remarkable powers of his mind to renew the Dutch Reformed church and to liberate the people of God in the Netherlands, together with their children, from a house of bondage. In his activities in both church and state, the cry of his heart was: "Let Christ be king!"

Reactions to the French Revolution

a. Restoration and conservatism

The great revolution and its Napoleonic aftermath had swept across the European family of nations, obliterating old institutions, customs and conceptions. Afterwards, many wanted to restore the former conditions in Europe. The first years after 1815 were years of *restoration*.

The restoration seemed to be embodied in the Holy Alliance of Czar Alexander I of Russia, and it found another incarnation in the Austrian diplomat von Metternich, who was said to have sought an immutable *status quo*. The first decades after the fall of Napoleon have been called the "age of Metternich."

The Holy Alliance, however, was not just an attempt to return to an earlier period of absolutism and aristocratic privilege. It was religiously inspired, for Czar Alexander had been deeply influenced by the pietistic baronness von Krüdener. His proclamation of the foundation and intentions of the Holy Alliance sound like a religious manifesto:

> Their majesties the emperor of Austria, the king of Prussia, and the emperor of Russia, having come to the heartfelt conviction that it is necessary to found the proper policy of the Powers in their mutual relationship on the lofty truths taught by the eternal religion of God the Redeemer, declare solemnly that it is the only purpose of the present decree to declare before the world that they intend to act, both in the government of their states and in their public relations to any other government, in agreement with the prescriptions of the holy religion, prescriptions of justice, love and peace which, far from being applicable to private life only, should influence the decisions of the princes and should direct all their steps, because they are the old means to preserve human institutions and to remedy their institutions.

Then follow the three principles of the Alliance. We read the following words:

> The three princes consider each other as delegates of Providence to reign over three branches of the same family, to wit Austria, Prussia and Russia, confessing that the Christian nation of which they and their peoples are a part in truth has no other Sovereign than He to whom belongs all power, because only in Him are found all treasures of love, knowledge and in-

finite wisdom; that is, our God, our divine Redeemer Jesus Christ, the Word of the Most High, the Word of life.[3]

These were high-sounding principles, and we cannot doubt the sincerity of the men who adopted them. But how were they to be applied? Where and how was the will of God for a nation to be found? Was the prince of a country the only one qualified to discover the real needs and to make the necessary laws?

In place of the absolutism of the pre-revolution period, the princes of the Holy Alliance established *paternalism* and the principle of *legitimism*. Paternalism at its very best meant that the princes wanted to be fathers to their people, but it also meant that they excluded the possibility that their subjects might have a say in ruling the affairs of the country. Legitimism meant that the given historical situation was willed by God and should therefore remain unchanged.

In this soil, nineteenth-century conservatism took root. Beginning in 1820, the influential French monthly *Le Conservateur*, in which Chateaubriand wrote important articles, defended the Bourbons and attacked the liberals. After 1830, the Tories in England were called the Conservatives. In Germany the conservatives were to be found among the gentry and the upper middle classes who supported Bismarck.

In The Netherlands of the nineteenth-century, many Christians supported the Conservative party, until about 1880. This party was characterized not so much by Christian principles as by the tendency to keep things as they were, which meant that it often fell prey to opportunism.

Kuyper lauded this conservatism for its love of the historical, but at the same time he declared that it was impossible for him and his followers to be conservative, explaining that he simply could not breathe in such an atmosphere. Moreover, he loathed the utilitarianism of the Conservatives, which subjected even the honor of the holy God to calculations of political advantage.[4]

b. Romanticism and historicism

Romanticism has been called a reaction to the rational elements of the French Revolution as well as a counterpart to its irrational elements.[5] In any case, it was surely a mighty current in European literature, art, philosophy, and theology in the first half of the nineteenth century, a current which stressed feeling over against reason, intuition over against intellect, and fantasy over against fixed ways of thinking.

In 1802 the French Romantic author de Chateaubriand published his *Génie du Christianisme, ou beautés de la religion Chrétienne (Genius of Christianity, or Beauties of the Christian Religion)*, in which he exclaimed: "Ma conviction est sortie du coeur; j'ai pleuré et j'ai cru" ("My conviction has sprung from the heart; I have cried and I have believed"). In this work he argued that history proves that the Christian faith was the main fountain of art and civilization in Europe. Under the inspiration of such Romanticism, many historical studies, biographies, reflections, and novels appeared. And only a single step separated this movement from historicism.

In our time the term *historicism* can mean the time-relatedness of all historical phenomena—their constant flux, changeability, and relativity.[6] The term can also be used to mean a philosophy of history.[7] I am using it here only to stand for the great interest in history that burgeoned in the first half of the nineteenth century under the influence of Romanticism. One of the causes and results of this interest in history was the republication of many ancient works.

Kuyper was influenced by romanticism and historicism. Despite his tendency toward stringent, consistent logical reasoning, his emotions played such a major role in his activities toward the end of his life that his enemies repeatedly accused him of being dramatic. His powerful imagination colored his speeches with vivid illustrations. Sometimes his fantasy overstepped the bounds of sober historical judgment.* He always became warmly enthusiastic when he spoke of patriotism or his love of the house of Orange, the Dutch monarchy.

He might have become one of the greatest historians of the nineteenth century if his work of reforming the church and calling the nation to the service of God had not absorbed his

---

* In his biographical sketch of the Anglo-Dutch theologian Alexander Comrie, which reads like a novel, Kuyper sometimes gives free rein to his imagination. See *The Catholic Presbyterian,* January, March and April 1882; see also A.G. Honig, *Alexander Comrie* (1892), pp. 19ff.

capacities. His publication of various works including the works of the Polish reformer a Lasco and the selected works of Junius and Voetius demonstrated his abilities in this field.

c. Réveil and orthodoxy

The European term *Réveil* reminds us of the English word *revival* and has similar connotations. Both refer to an awakening of spiritual life; however, a revival usually takes place in a certain city or part of a country and lasts only for a limited period of time, but the Réveil appeared in several areas of Europe (Switzerland, France, Germany, The Netherlands, and Scotland) at about the same time (the first half of the nineteenth century) and had some lasting effects. It was the reaction of a slumbering orthodoxy against the prevailing rationalism and liberalism of the time. Although it manifested pietistic and individualistic tendencies, it set out to reform the churches, not to secede from them.

Extreme liberalism reigned supreme in Geneva at the time when a young minister named César Malan preached in 1817 on a subject that was unusual for the time: "Man can be saved only by Jesus Christ." He was deposed from office. From then on the theme of his sermon was one of the forbidden topics in Geneva's church (along with original sin and predestination).

Since Malan did not want to establish a new church, he met with followers in his own house. He considered the chapel that was built later and the congregation that met in the chapel to be part of the national church. But it was almost inevitable that in 1849 a Free Evangelical Church was established. It was preceded in 1847 by the Free Evangelical Church of the Pays de Vaud, with Alexandre Vinet taking a leadership position.

Vinet had been converted to Christ after an almost fatal illness. He was a powerful preacher of the gospel; however he founded his theology not on the infallible word of Scripture but on the pure voice of the human conscience. Kuyper opposed this way of thinking when it appeared in The Netherlands as Ethical theology.

The most famous name connected with the Réveil in France was that of Adolphe Monod, who was deposed from his office in the Reformed church of Lyons in 1832 by his liberal consistory. He was a most eloquent preacher of the grace of Christ.

Two features marked his special position in the Réveil. In the first place, he did not want to see a rupture in the Reformed church; even after a free church was founded he did not want separation. Secondly, although he accepted the inspiration of the Bible, under the influence of Vinet, he wavered on this position.

In Germany the Réveil was called the "Erweckungsbewegung." The starting signal for this movement was given by Claus Harms, a minister in Kiel, who republished Luther's ninety-five theses on the 31st of October, 1817, and added to them ninety-five of his own. The ninth of his own theses read: "The pope of our time, in view of faith, is reason; in view of works it is conscience." The theologian of this awakening was Prof. A. Tholuck, who attacked the coldness of rationalism in his *Doctrine of Sin and of the Redeemer.*

It is a remarkable fact that in this period two converted Jews gave leadership to the Evangelical community in Germany. One was J.A.W. Neander (original name: David Mendel), who wrote an extensive history of the church. The other was F.J. Stahl (original name: F.J. Jolson), a jurist who held high office in the state's ecclesiastical organization and wanted to realize the ideal of a Christian state in Prussia. Stahl influenced both Groen van Prinsterer and Abraham Kuyper, although Kuyper also underscored certain words once spoken by Groen: "Stahl was a Lutheran; I am a Calvinist."[8]

In Scotland the names of Robert Haldane and Thomas Chalmers stand out. Haldane, who was first attracted by the ideas of the French Revolution, was converted in 1794 and started preaching wherever he had the opportunity. In 1816 he went to Geneva and was behind the first impulses toward the Réveil in that city.

Chalmers was minister in Glasgow from 1815 to 1823 and a professor thereafter. In 1843 he began to serve as leader of the Free Church of Scotland. His activities in the church and in social and political life remind one of the subsequent energetic labors of Abraham Kuyper in The Netherlands. As a minister he organized the relief for the poor and improved the physical, moral and spiritual conditions of the underprivileged in the city. He revived the office of deacon and founded Sunday schools and day schools. He wanted freedom for the church especially with respect to patronage. When parliament maintained patronage, which meant that the local churches were not free to call their own ministers, Chalmers and his followers left the General Assembly of the Scottish Presbyterian Church and founded the Free Church of Scotland. "With great enthusiasm and much sacrifice the laity of the Free Church erected new buildings, supported their ministers and organized for the initiation and support of foreign missions."[9]

The most important representative of the Dutch Réveil was Guillaume Groen van Prinsterer. For years he was a lonely warrior in the Dutch parliament, where he tried to apply Christian principles to political life. Groen had been converted through the preaching of Merle d'Audigné, a Swiss son of the Réveil, who had been brought to the faith of his fathers through the preaching of the Scotsman Haldane. In his famous work *Unbelief and Revolution*, Groen attacked the ideas of the French Revolution, which he viewed as an embodiment of the unbelieving spirit of the eighteenth-century Enlightenment.

All his life Groen struggled for the reformation of the state church and against liberty of doctrine in that church. He also fought for the authority of the Word of God in public life. As a member of the House of Commons he called himself "not a statesman, but a proclaimer of the gospel." At the end of his life he greeted Kuyper as his talented successor, who would reap where he himself had sown.

The men of the Dutch Réveil kept themselves rather aloof from the Secession (*Afscheiding*) from the state church that took place in 1834 under the guidance of such courageous young preachers as H. de Cock and S. van Velzen. They spoke up for these men when they were persecuted and showed them their sympathy, but they remained with the old national church.

The men of the Dutch Réveil were evangelical members of the aristocracy, whereas the men of the Secession belonged mainly to the lower classes of society. To the chagrin of Groen, the men of the Réveil were also rather conservative in their political and social ideals, whereas the Secessionists were more consistently Calvinistic.

In line with the Revolution

a. Liberalism

We should be careful in our use of the term *liberalism*, for it has more than one meaning. In its many uses, the word connotes the attractive notion of human freedom—freedom from bonds, from traditions, from authority. Theologically speaking, it denotes the trend toward human autonomy which we find in many nineteenth- and twentieth-century churches. Rejecting the traditional views of the authority of the Bible and the confessions, the liberals proclaimed the supremacy of human reason, experience, or feeling. Politically speaking, the word *liberal* stands for the organization that grew out of the old Whig party in England and Canada. In the United States the term is applied to members or sectors of political parties that wish to be more progressive than the others.

I am using the term *liberalism* here to stand for the philosophy of the members of the nineteenth-century European middle classes who wished to apply the principles of the French Revolution in a moderate way. These liberals detested the Reign of Terror and the extravagances of the Revolution, but they accepted without reserve the great principles of the Revolution—the autonomy of man and of human reason, independent of any divine revelation.

The difference between such liberals and orthodox Christians was summed up in the following words by the Dutch liberal statesman S. van Houten:

> We acknowledge neither a revelation as the source of our knowledge of truth and justice nor the authority of any agency of the church. In the light of reason alone, we observe the expressions of the will of the people in the present and in the past. We assess its conceivable consequences and try to promote happiness and prosperity while averting grief. Not a so-called "word of God" but (in the language of the believers) the gift of God which we possess in our reason is the lamp to our feet.[10]

Liberalism was in favor of the sovereignty of the people—but not of all the people. It wanted sovereignty for the middle classes, the bourgeoisie, but not for the working class or the proletariat. That was why the liberals restricted the franchise to citizens who paid at least a certain specified amount in taxes.

The economic wisdom of the liberals was summarized in their slogan, "Laissez faire, laissez aller," which meant that in the age of industrialization thousands of workers were allowed to live in the poorest of conditions. In the name of this slogan, women and children were exploited for profit.

The liberals were tolerant with respect to all sorts of opinions that deviated from the Word of God, but they were intolerant toward orthodox groups that wanted freedom of worship, as became apparent in the days of the Secession (*Afscheiding*) in The Netherlands in 1834. They promoted up-to-date education for the children of the nation in state-controlled schools but insisted that no genuine Christian doctrine be taught. And they made the establishment of free Christian schools almost impossible.

Most of Abraham Kuyper's public activities were to be devoted to a continuing struggle against liberalism in church, state and society. He became the great champion of a free church, of free Christian schools with the same rights and duties as public schools, and of sound social legislation on behalf of the so-called little people (*kleine luyden*).

b. Socialism and Communism

The nineteenth century was also the age of the rise of Marxism, the philosophy that proclaimed the doctrine of the class struggle and produced proletarian socialism and elitist Communism. Marxism was a legitimate child of liberalism. It, too, struggled for liberty, equality and fraternity (apart from Jesus Christ), but not for a certain class of well-to-do, well-mannered and well-meaning middle-class citizens; its battle was especially on behalf of the large group of the under-privileged—the proletariat.

Marxism denied and opposed the authority of the Word of God in a more radical way than liberalism had done. It started with the slogan "Religion belongs to private life," but it showed its real colors when it proclaimed: "Religion is the opium of the people."

Liberalism had promoted a materialistic outlook on life. It considered all labor merchandise which was liable to the law of supply and demand. Liberalism liked to speak of the iron law of wages: the wages of the workers could not be higher than what it cost a working-class family to live.

Marxism was *completely* materialistic. In this system, all human relationships, ideals and religions are merely the reflection of material circumstances. Hence there is a constant and unavoidable class struggle underway. And every class of people creates its own morality and sticks to its own prejudices. The only way to bring this endless struggle to an end is to promote the classless society. The coming of such a society was prophesied with messianic fervor; it would be the glorious outcome of a terrible worldwide revolution.

The first socialists of the nineteenth century (the name *socialism* came into use about 1830) have been called utopian socialists. Yet some of them offered practical programs (e.g. Fourier, Louis Blanc).

In 1848 Marx and Engels issued their *Communist Manifesto,* in which they advocated the sharing of wealth in such a manner that the private ownership of the means of production would be abolished. The *Manifesto* ended with these flaming words:

> The Communists disdain to conceal their views and aims. They openly declare that their ends can be attained only by the forcible overthrow of all existing social conditions. Let the ruling classes tremble at a Communist revolution. The proletarians have nothing to lose but their chains. They have a world to win. Working men of all countries, unite!

There were many reasons why the socialist and Communist appeal struck a responsive chord. The situation of the workers in many industrial centers and agricultural areas was more than deplorable.

Kuyper opposed socialism, but he was well aware of the real challenge it represented. He planned and pleaded for the improvement of social conditions and for Christian labor organizations.

c. Evolutionism

Evolutionism is older than Darwin. Already in 1796 Laplace had plublished his book *L'exposition du système de monde*, in which he tried to derive the existence of the solar system without mentioning the name of God. When Napoleon asked him the reason for this startling omission, he replied:

"Sire, je n'avais pas besoin de cette hypothèse" (Sir, I didn't need that hypothesis).

In Laplace's opinion, then, God was merely a hypothesis which one might or might not need. Gradually this became the position of Charles Darwin (1809-1882), the prophet of evolutionism. When he made his famous journey on the "Beagle," Darwin still considered himself a Christian, and he quoted the Bible with regard to ethical questions. But in time he found that he could no longer accept the miracles of the Bible, especially that of creation. His increasing knowledge of what he regarded as the unchangeable laws of nature made such faith impossible for him.

In 1859 Darwin published his famous book *The Origin of Species,* which proposed three main theses. He maintained that within certain areas of the biological world, at least, a gradual evolution has taken place from simpler to more complex organisms. He explained that this evolution was guided by "natural selection," by which he meant the survival of the fittest in the struggle for existence. Finally, he maintained that the origins of the human race were to be found in the animal world.

The idea of gradual evolution spread like wildfire. It was applied not only in biology and the natural sciences generally but also in linguistics, law, psychology, sociology, economics, and the various departments of theology:

> The history of Israel could be understood as the gradual evolving of the Hebrew religious consciousness, from the simple and crude conceptions of the earliest writings to the exalted monotheism of the prophets. As God had brought man into existence through a long evolutionary process, so He had progressively revealed Himself to man, with the climax being reached in Christ. A similar pattern of explanation was widely accepted in the study of the history of religions (or "comparative religions"), which came into prominence about the beginning of the twentieth century.[11]

Evolutionism is an important part of the pattern of the nineteenth century. It was the age of the refined historical method, which boasted a thorough study of sources and a concomitant rejection of many traditional conceptions as fables, legends or myths. It was the age of the great expansion of the white race, of the discovery of the heart of Africa, and of the study of the languages and customs of primitive peoples. It was

the age of great industrial development, which seemed to promise a future of unlimited prosperity, it was an age without significant world wars, an age enjoying a moderate measure of peace.

In a word, the nineteenth century was an age of great expectations, of optimism. It seemed to spell the dawn of a new time
and of a new man. At the end of this century, the great
philosopher Nietzsche was to scorn the spirit of his time. But he
could also speak with expectation of the coming superman
(*Uebermensch*), the laughing lion.

Kuyper was confronted with the idea of evolution in various
ways. In 1899 he spoke the famous words: "Our nineteenth century dies away under the hypnosis of the dogma of Evolution."[14]

An important thinker of the nineteenth century was Ludwig
Feuerbach (1804-1872), a radical atheist. His book, *The Essence
of Christianity,* presents Christianity as an illusion, and the idea
of God as a projection of the human mind. Feuerbach influenced Nietzsche, who proclaimed the death of God and
wanted to abolish all the values derived from Christianity. Feuerbach also influenced Marx and Engels, the fathers of Communism, and became the official theologian of the Soviet Communists.

The most famous Dutch atheist of the nineteenth century
was Multatuli (the pen name of E. Douwes Dekker who wrote
many volumes of "Ideas"). In "De Dageraad" (The Dawn), an
association of freethinkers, he was hailed as "Master
Multatuli." This association was fanatically opposed to any and
all forms of religion and succeeded in estranging many workers
from the church.

The term *agnosticism* was coined during this same period in
England by T.H. Huxley (1825-1895), who with the term made
reference to Acts 17:23. Huxley was convinced that man is
unable to fathom the nature of either spirit or matter.
Metaphysics is then an impossibility, and man's primary duty in
life is to try to remedy misery and ignorance.

The French form of this agnosticism is to be found in the
positivism of Comte (1798-1857), who wanted to remove
metaphysics completely from the domain of knowledge. According to Comte, we can know and order only the phenomena
of our experience. In the final period of his life Comte invented
a religion without God, a religion which venerates the heroes
and great men of humankind.

Chapter 2

Trial and Error:
Theology of the Time

Rationalism

In the first half of the nineteenth century, representatives of old-fashioned rationalism were still influential. In the formerly pietistic University of Halle, rationalism was expounded by Julius Wegscheider (1771-1849). His book of 1815, *Institutiones Theologiae Christianae Dogmaticae,* went through eight editions and was the standard dogmatics handbook of the time. With a naive trust in human reason, Wegscheider replaced the principle of the Reformation (redemption by faith through the grace of Christ) with the principle of the self-redemption of man, with Jesus serving as example.[1]

In a similar commentary on one of the gospels, H.E.G. Paulus (1761-1851) described Christ's resurrection as an awakening from an apparent death. He maintained that when Jesus was said to be walking on the water, he was really walking along the coast. Such thinking was an outgrowth of eighteenth-century convictions, and it was always in the background of nineteenth century liberal thinking.

Schleiermacher, who will be discussed later, certainly did not want to be called a rationalist; yet when Freiherr von Stein expressed the wish that some strong measures be taken against "a dozen rationalists who should be expelled from their status docendi," Schleiermacher published a letter in which he declared that, after having heard of fixed doctrinal principles, he felt like one "who was all of a sudden surrounded by darkness and had to grope for the door in order to come back to the free light."[2]

In 1832 the following rationalistic confession was framed by J.F. Róhr, the court chaplain of Weimar:

> There is a true God whom we should wholeheartedly worship as the most perfect of all beings, as the Creator, Provider and Governor of the World, and as the Father of mankind. This worship consists primarily in striving for virtue and honesty, in industrious struggle against sensuous urges and passions, and in reasonable devotion to duty according to the example of Jesus. Conscious of this, we may be comforted by the fatherly help of God in all distress of this world, by His grace and mercy in the feeling of our moral unworthiness, and by a better and blessed life after the moment of our death.[3]

A similar rationalism was prevalent in The Netherlands during this period. Groen van Prinsterer described it in the following words:

> Christ, God revealed in the flesh, was called a divine Being higher than the other creatures; the Holy Spirit was nothing but a divine power; original sin was moral corruption, weakness, imperfection, perfectibility; in the suffering and death of the Mediator no more than a proof of God's common love to mankind was acknowledged; regeneration, conversion and sanctification were transformed into moral improvement and the beginning and progress of the practice of virtue; and heaven was opened to all who did not commit gross outward sins.[4]

Kuyper was later to write of "the curse of Rationalism which succeeded in chilling to the bone all churches on the continent, with the exception of the Dutch ones."[5] He was willing to make this one exception because he was also writing about Alexander Comrie, the Dutch-Scottish minister of Woubrugge, who protested against the spirit of the time and was a stalwart Calvinist.

Kuyper was right to speak of rationalism as a freezing winter wind. Yet he described the Dutch situation too optimistically, for despite the efforts of Comrie and others, it had not escaped the chill either.

Supernaturalism

The most unavoidable orthodox counterpart of rationalism was supernaturalism, which tried to demonstrate that God's revelation is reasonably supernatural. The fact of revelation was taken for granted, but the possibility and necessity of natural theology was also assumed. All possible efforts were made to demonstrate that there is agreement between the rational insights of man and the revealed truth of God.

The English bishop Butler was a pioneer in this field. To a certain extent, the Dutch theologians Munthinge and Van Oosterzee followed in his footsteps. Bishop Butler (1692-1752) wrote a book entitled *Analogy of Religion, Natural and Revealed* (1736), in which he argued for comformity between the two forms of religion. His main argument was based on *probability* and *security:* although we must concede, he argued, that the Christian religion cannot be demonstrated in a mathematical way, we must immediately add that our conclusions in other fields are marked by probability as well. In such a situation there is more security to be found in following the prescriptions of God's revealed truth than in neglecting them.

H. Munthinge (1752-1824), a Groningen professor, tried to demonstrate the reasonableness of God's revelation by pointing to its progressive character, its adaptation to the degree of human development, and its education of the human race. He criticized the doctrine of Christ's satisfaction of God's wrath as "an unworthy and unreasonable idea" and even called it blasphemous.[6]

The Dutch apologist J.J. van Oosterzee (1817-1882) was certainly not a supernaturalist in the vulgar sense of the term, in fact, he was equally opposed to "the banal meanness of supernaturalism and that of rationalism."[7] With all his heart Van Oosterzee brought the message of the manger and the cross. Yet he was the founder and main representative of a school of apologetics that depended on reason to establish the facts of revelation. The result was that every now and then he deviated from the confession of the Reformed church. Occasionally he opposed Kuyper, to whom he wrote in 1873: "We cannot change the facts: we are fundamentally opposed to each other . . . let me part from you with a handshake of appreciation."[8]

Men like Van Oosterzee tried to defend the essential values of Christianity. The defense they offered, however, was too rationalistic to be of real value in the great battle against the rising tide of modernism.

Schleiermacher and his school

Schleiermacher was a man of his time; to a certain extent, he was *the* theologian of his time. Earlier I spoke of the Romantic movement as a necessary reaction to rationalism; to a certain extent and during a certain period of his life, Schleiermacher was the theologian of that movement.

The church historian Neander said of Schleiermacher after his death: "With him will begin a new period in the history of the church." Karl Barth, who raised his mighty voice against Schleiermacher's subjectivistic theology, could not refrain from praising him as "a hero only rarely given to theology." Barth added: "In the field of theology it was *his* age."[9]

Even Kuyper, who had protested with all his might against Schleiermacher's pantheism,[10] praised him on a later occasion in the following words:

> When he appeared on the scene, he found sacred theology almost strangled by the cord of philosophy, lying in an out-of-the-way corner of the cemetery, sparsely adorned by some hesitating friends with flowers plucked from history and humanism. Theology had followed the way of religion, and both had lost their prestige. All things connected with the church or with church life were in a state of confusion. But that was exactly what Schleiermacher could not tolerate any longer. In his view religious life was a jewel that adorned his own soul, the breath of life for the people of the church. He wanted to restore the honor of that religion, and because that honor could not be recaptured as long as it could not lift its head with scientific self-respect among the cultured of the German nation, it was his ambition—indeed, his jealousy—to create for her a theology that made its voice heard.[11]

Kuyper used these words to sketch the desolate position of theology at the beginning of the nineteenth century. In the minds of many at that time, rationalism had destroyed the possibility and validity of any supernatural revelation. Supernaturalism strove in vain to defend positions that were already lost.

Followers of Kant tried to preserve a place for religion as a postulate of reason, but they replaced the knowledge and service of God with the obligation to listen to the voice of duty; in other words, they allowed morality to usurp the place of religion. As for Romanticism, it returned with nostalgia to the fields of venerable history, but in the process it often moved from religion to aesthetics: religion, it proclaimed, touches our emotions in the same way as a painting of Rembrandt or the imposing cathedral in Cologne.

This was the climate in which Schleiermacher breathed day by day. In response, he wrote his *Address on Religion to Its Cultured Despisers*, in which he exclaimed:

> Religion is not knowledge and science, either of the world or of God. Without being knowledge, it recognizes knowledge and science. In itself it is an affection, a revelation of the Infinite in the finite, God being seen in it and it in God.[12]

Religion, then, was an affection, a feeling. As Barth put it: "Schleiermacher's theology is a theology of feeling—or more precisely, a theology of pious feeling. Or it is a theology of consciousness—or more precisely, a theology of pious consciousness."[13]

In these *Addresses* Schleiermacher came very close to Romanticism, which expressed itself in terms of feeling and aesthetic sensation. Yet his own notion of feeling had a special religious character. In a later systematic work he called it "the feeling of absolute dependence."

It has been said that Schleiermacher did not form a school.[14] However, it has also been stated that all theology after him is dependent on him: "His dogmatics was adopted by no one; yet he influenced all the schools of theological thought—liberal, moderate, confessional—and all the churches—Roman Catholic, Lutheran and Reformed. Most closely allied to him were the so-called 'mediating theologians' (*Vermittlungstheologen*)."[15]

The followers of Schleiermacher were of two sorts. On the one hand Schleiermacher has been called "the father of modern theology."[16] Many theologians stressed the subjective elements of his theology so strongly as to abolish all traces of supernatural revelation. In this way they tried to keep pace with the modern consciousness.

There was also a right wing; many orthodox theologians were also influenced by Schleiermacher. They wanted to defend the content of the Bible and of confessional standards, but did so by appealing to human feelings or to the echo the Bible and the confessions evoked in the human heart. These theologians were also somewhat critical of Scripture. It was exactly here that Kuyper was to speak his inexorable *no* even to his former semi-orthodox friends.

English theology in this period

The spirit of the time not only pervaded the continent of Europe but was also in the air in England and Scotland. We noted that the Swiss Réveil was rooted in Scotland, and spoke of how Chalmers and his followers reacted against the eighteenth-century traditionalism of the Church of Scotland.

During this period, Coleridge was writing in England, a poet sometimes called the English Schleiermacher. F.D. Maurice was representative of more progressive Christian social ideas. J.H. Newman and his somewhat Romantic Oxford movement kindled new interest in the origin and historical background of the Church of England.

Samuel Taylor Coleridge (1772-1834) was in his poetry as Romantic as Southey and Wordsworth. He also wrote religious works which show the influence of the German philosopher Kant and the German poet Goethe. Coleridge presents religion as essentially ethical; practical reason is the source of our religious knowledge. Redemption is an ethical act of man—not an objective act of God.

Coleridge formed no school, but he did influence many of the younger theologians. He has been called "the originator of the Broad-church or liberal movement in the Church of England, which was so striking a feature of the nineteenth century."[17]

Frederick Denison Maurice (1805-1872), the son of a Unitarian minister, turned to the Anglican church and was mainly orthodox. However, he eventually resigned from his office as theological professor under suspicion of heresy because of his sentiments on the question of eternal punishment. With his friends Kingsley and Ludlow, he started the Christian socialist movement, which was directed against the "laissez faire" principles of liberalism. In 1850 he and his friends opened cooperative workshops for tailoring, building, iron-founding, and other crafts. In 1854 he established a "Working Man's College," in which he himself became a professor. The movement he started met with much hostility, but it exercised a lasting influence on the Church of England and promoted the formation of trade unions and education for the working class.

Kuyper had studied the works of Maurice, and in one of his first speeches in the Dutch House of Commons he referred to "his brilliant talent and comprehensive activities."[18] He also sympathized with John Henry Newman (1801-1890), who yearned for a real church, a mother for believers and "a pillar and bulwark of the truth."

The difference between these two great church leaders was that Newman looked for his ideal in notions of the ancient church and finally found his ideals realized in the Roman Catholic Church, whereas Kuyper rediscovered the treasures of the Reformation and tried to realize his ideals in a truly Reformed church. They both wanted unity of doctrine and life; Newman found such unity in the tradition and practice of the Roman Catholic Church, while Kuyper found it in Holy Scripture and in the confessions of faith of the Reformation period, which he wanted to see expressed and applied in the language and life of the people of his time.

Chapter 3

The Dutch Situation

The Church and Churches

The Dutch Reformed Church had been the privileged state church for two centuries before the time of the Revolution. Then a decree of 1796, confirmed in the Constitution of 1798, proclaimed the equality of all existing religious communities and established the principle of the separation of church and state.

In actual fact, a number of churches were coexisting before then, even though membership in the established church was a requirement for holding public office. The Netherlands had long been one of the most tolerant countries in Europe. Roman Catholics had their clandestine churches (*schuilkerken*) in various places and even made up the bulk of the population in the so-called "Lands of the Generality" (the present provinces of Brabant and Limburg). Since 1724, there had been an Old Catholic Church, independent of Rome. There was also a fraternity of Mennonites, made up of many churches, especially in the province of Friesland, to say nothing of a Remonstrant Society and various Lutheran churches.

Each of these churches and church groups had once possessed its own character, but the ideas of the eighteenth-century Enlightenment had wreaked havoc with their professional standards and convictions. All the churches except for the Roman Catholic Church had been drawn together by the nationalism and moralism of the time.

Another unifying force was the influence exercised by the sovereign of The Netherlands, William I, who was a cousin of Frederick William III, the Prussian king who united the Lutheran and Reformed churches in his own country in 1817. Before the Dutch king was restored to the throne of his fathers, he had ruled some smaller German states, where he grew accustomed to taking a paternal attitude toward his subjects—the attitude of an enlightened monarch.[1]

William wanted to rule The Netherlands as a God-given king, and he felt called to settle the matter of the church in an appropriate way. His right-hand man was Janssen, the Secretary of State. Their leading idea was to unite all Protestant citizens in one Protestant church. The eventual result was the abrogation of the freedom of the Dutch Reformed Church. A royal decree was introduced in 1816, replacing the old synodical system of church government by a new system in which the king appointed the members of the General Synod.

In establishing this arrangement, the king had two goals in mind. In the first place, he wanted to be a good Christian king. After all, he lived in the days of the Holy Alliance. He wanted to be a father to his people, who would then live in Christian unity as members of the nation's one church. In the second place, he wanted unified administration for the church.

He never intended *unity in doctrine*. He may have hoped that it would come about gradually, but for the time being he wished that all the members of the church would tolerate all the others when it came to questions of doctrine. Therefore the royal decree contained a new form of subscription for office-bearers, which was different from the one that had been used until then; from now on the candidates for office would have to declare that they accepted and believed "the doctrine contained in the accepted Forms of Unity in accordance with the Word of God."

These words could be interpreted in either an orthodox way or a liberal way. They could mean that the confessional standards of the church should be accepted *because (quia)* they were in accordance with the Word of God, but they could also mean that they should be accepted *in so far as* (*quatenus*) they were in agreement with the Word. Because both viewpoints were possible, the laxer of the two won the day. From then on, freedom of doctrine would be the hallmark of the Dutch Reformed Church.

In later years Kuyper pointed out how the signing of the confessions had become a mere formality. N.C. Kist, his much respected professor of church history, had printed in a Dutch historical magazine a reproduction of the signatures of the

Leiden professors of his time under the Canons of Dort, even though two of those professors had publicly repudiated the Canons (as Kist himself had also done). Calling this "a puzzling signature" and "a psychological problem," Kuyper noted that merely signing one's name was not a guarantee of faithfulness.[2]

The royal decree of King William occasioned protests and disruption. Classis Amsterdam protested first against the new ecclesiastical arrangement, and seven other classes followed its example. All of these classes were dissolved, and thus the mouths of the protestants were silenced.

In 1834 a secession (*afscheiding*) disrupted the king's proud unified order. Young ministers in various parts of the country joined to ask synod to uphold sound doctrine and to resist heresy. They were either deposed from office or—in the case of candidates—not admitted to the ministry at all. After they started free churches of a genuinely Reformed character, they were opposed, suppressed and persecuted by the tolerant liberals of their time. Yet their churches persevered and multiplied: after fifty years their membership amounted to some 300,000 people.

A number of them eventually emigrated to the United States, under the leadership of Van Raalte and Scholte, two of their ministers. Among those emigrants were the founding fathers of the Christian Reformed Church of North America.

Theology and theologians

The European ideas of the nineteenth century did not pass The Netherlands by. The great movement known as the Réveil took on its own Dutch national character when men like Da Costa and Groen van Prinsterer protested against the spirit of the age, and when the "Christian Friends" met regularly to discuss the situation of the church and the nation. The strength of the Dutch Réveil was that when these men stood up and were counted, some of them wanted to confess the kingship of Christ in church, state and society. Its weakness, on the other hand, was its rather aristocratic constituency; it did not reach out to the common man. It lacked consistency and harbored a variety of theological opinions.

At the time of the Réveil, there were all kinds of other

theological persuasions in The Netherlands. In one of his first publications, Kuyper offers a survey; he speaks of "Groningers, Evangelicals, followers of the Leiden school, Old Moderns, Young Moderns, Empiricals, Ethicals, Criticals, Irenicals, Confessionals, Friends of the Truth, Kohlbruggians, Followers of De Liefde, of Irving, of Darby, Baptists, and more of the same." Then he goes on to make the interesting observation that most of these divisions are caused more by persons than by principles. "Groningen," he writes, "is Hofstede de Groot, Leiden is Scholten, the Ethicals is De La Saussaye, the Empiricals is Opzoomer, the Criticals is Doedes, the Confessionals is Felix, the Irenicals is Cramer."[3]

It would carry us too far afield to discuss these eleven groups separately. I will deal with only three of them, the three which we will encounter again—the Groningers, the Ethicals and the Moderns.

a. The Groningers

When Schleiermacher's star began to rise over Germany, the University of Groningen produced a group of young theologians who pleaded, like Schleiermacher, for a theology of the heart. Yet their leader, Hofstede de Groot, could declare in all honesty: "We did not become acquainted with Schleiermacher until our theology had already taken on its special character."[4]

Their theology was marked by warmth of feeling, by a deep respect for Jesus Christ as the great Educator of the human race, and by a great optimism: the educational process would go on and on and would eventually reunite all real Christians. The Groningers emphasized the national character of their movement and claimed as their heroes not John Calvin and the fathers of Dort but the Dutch Christian humanists Erasmus and Hugo Grotius.

The Groningen theology was essentially a Christian humanism with a strong emphasis on the human personality of Christ. In Christology it was Arian; in anthropology it was Pelagian. Although it rejected rationalistic criticism of Scripture, it did not accept the absolute authority of the Word of

God. It objected to the term *infallibility*, speaking of "faultlessness" instead.

This interesting point of view might be characterized as a halfway position. "No infallibility!" said the Groningers, because to claim infallibility would be to make a dogmatic, *a priori* statement about a human book. All the same, Groningers were able to ascribe "faultlessness" to the Bible. This was a scientific, *a posteriori* judgment at which the Groningers arrived after having studied the Bible, especially the New Testament. The weakness of their position became evident as soon as nineteenth century "scientific" Bible criticism began to cut to pieces one Bible book after another.

When Kuyper was born, the Groningen theology was prevalent in The Netherlands. It was preached from almost all the pulpits of the state church, especially in the province of Groningen; indeed, its prevalence was one of the reasons why the Secession (*Afscheiding*) spread in that province. Yet the fruits of this Christian humanism were very disappointing. In 1862, a disciple of this school expressed his disappointment about the situation of the church in the province of Groningen in the following words:

> The Lord's Supper is celebrated regularly, but in a large part of the province there are few confessing members; the solemnization of marriage in the church is desired only by a few; religious life in the families is at a low ebb; a very worldly walk of life prevails; drunkenness and immorality are terribly bad among the workers; generally speaking, there is little respect for church life, for the church, or for its servants.[5]

In 1868, Kuyper collided head-on with the Groningen theology. That year, to celebrate the third centennial of the Convent of Wesel,* a conference was held in Zeist in which Dutch and German theologians participated. He protested against the fact that the leadership of the conference was in the hands of the Groningers, who had deviated so much from the principles of the fathers. Kuyper pushed for a celebration in the style of the fathers—not in the style of the Pharisees who built tombs for the prophets after having killed them. Although he was hissed down

---

* The first semi-synodical meeting of the Dutch Reformed churches of the Reformation.

at the meeting, he had given the starting signal for a lifelong battle to establish clear-cut and honest relationships and celebrations in the church of Jesus Christ.

b. *The Ethical theology*

It was only a single step from the Groningen theology to radical modernism. The theologians who refused to take that step, even though they remained opposed to classical Reformed orthodoxy, were the proponents of the Ethical theology. These men were the Dutch representatives of what was known in Germany as "Vermittlungstheologie" (mediating theology).

They were influenced by Schleiermacher, but not exclusively by him. They sympathized with the Réveil to a certain extent, and especially with Vinet, the man who appealed to the human conscience. Their broadly European outlook is evident from the fact that some of them were among the first to appreciate the lonesome Danish thinker Soren Kierkegaard. On the other hand they were definitely *Dutch* theologians. Their moderation was in keeping with the Dutch national character, which is averse to extremes and inclined to appreciate different points of view simultaneously.

The father of the Ethical theology in The Netherlands was Daniel Chantepie de la Saussaye (1818-1874). His most devout disciple was Johannes Hermanus Gunning (1829-1905). Many talented theologians belonged to their group. From 1853 on, they published their ideas in a magazine called *Ernst en Vrede* (Earnestness and Peace).

These Ethical theologians have been called the existentialists of their time.[6] This characterization may be a caricature, but it cannot be denied that they reacted to the rationalism and supernaturalism of their time in a way that reminds us of Kierkegaard's contemporaneous protest against all human "systems." It was Chantepie's avowed conviction that the acceptance of an orthodox system and the use of certain orthodox terms was not yet proof of a living faith, for the character of the truth is not rational but "ethical." He did not use the term *ethical* to mean moral or moralistic; what he meant was "the deeper area of the inner personal life."[7]

An ethical truth—what might this mean with respect to the

authority of the Bible? To say that the Bible's authority is ethical means that the human form of this book is vulnerable to all varieties of lower and higher criticism. However, as soon as the Bible touches our conscience, it is God's living Word.

What does this outlook mean with respect to other points of doctrine? Let us listen to the description given by Herman Bavinck:

> Over against Athanasius, Arius was somewhat in the right, as we should now acknowledge; we cannot deny that Athanasius's doctrine of the Trinity was insufficient as far as the ethical relation between the Father and the Son is concerned. Likewise, Pelagius was somewhat in the right with respect to the insufficiency of Augustine's doctrine of predestination, for Pelagius aimed to explain—to some degree, at least—the fact of human conscience and the reality of the feeling of responsibility and guilt. Moreover, there is no absolute contrast between Catholicism and Protestantism. The same is true with respect to the Rationalism and Supernaturalism of the eighteenth century. It is impossible for de la Saussaye to join either Confessionalism or Modernism.[8]

The Ethicals were often called "Irenicals." They could put up with people in the church who denied even the great facts of salvation. However, they could hardly abide the activities of their good friend Groen van Prinsterer when he fought his lonely battle in the Dutch parliament to reform the schools, renew society, and withstand the spirit of revolution. And when Kuyper, Groen's successor, emphasized the necessity of a Christian political party and of all kinds of Christian activity even more strongly, he was constantly opposed and disparaged by these "irenical" Christians. They opposed any notion of antithesis, desiring a synthesis on an ethical basis with all well-meaning elements in the Dutch nation.

c. Modern theology

In his student years, Kuyper had been an enthusiastic disciple of the proponents of the Modern theology. The Moderns, as their name suggests, wanted to be men of the present, not of the past. The same claim had been made by men of the eighteenth-century Enlightenment, and it would later be made by proponents of the "new theology" in the twentieth century.

The Moderns lived in an age when natural science could point to great triumphs. Historical criticism of the original biblical sources became a project for theology. The rising middle class was "sold" to the idea of continuing human progress, while the theory of evolution continued to penetrate and influence society.

In such a time, a problem that had confronted Schleiermacher was knocking with new power at the door of the church: Is there still a little corner left for faith? What is the relation between faith and science? Is it possible for us to be men of our time *and* men of the Bible, to be living and active men of our age *and* loyal, faithful members of the church?

J.H. Scholten (1811-1885), the grand master of Dutch Modernism, looked these questions squarely in the face and

> when he prophesied from his chair, with students from all the faculties (of the university) listening to him, he carried his entire audience far above the towers of the villages of our country, for he testified that the more fearless we are in making use of the gift of God in our scientific judgment, the more brightly God will ultimately enlighten us with His truth. Scholten's students declared that he supported them in the enormous crisis of their days.[9]

The young Scholten had begun with Groningen theology, but found he could not agree with its doctrine of the faultlessness of the Bible. He rejected external authority in favor of inner authority, finding that in what he called the testimony of the Holy Spirit.

But his Modernist streak also came out; he used this venerable Calvinistic[10] and confessional[11] term to undergird his own man-centered theology of authority. He warned against three dangers as he talked about the testimony of the Holy Spirit. First, no one should suppose that this testimony supports the *authority* of Scripture; it only underscores the *value* of Scripture. Secondly, no one should suppose that this testimony relates to all the contents of Scripture; it witnesses only with regard to Scripture's *truly religious* parts. Thirdly, no one should make the mistake of thinking that this testimony bears a supernatural or immediate character; rather, it should be described as "the testimony of reason and conscience, purified by the Christian mind."[12]

All this maneuvering of Scholten means simply that he uses orthodox terms in order to bolster *un*orthodox opinions. While seeming to uphold the authority of the Word of God and of the confessions of the Reformed churches, he in fact undermines that authority. It was not for nothing that he called himself "an apostle of Reason."[13]

Scholten's deterministic conception of God, corresponded in many respects with the God of Spinoza, whom he revered. To Scholten, God was the harmonizing and organizing power of the universe, whose providence coincides with the laws of nature. Miracles are impossible, for nature cannot contradict itself. Jesus was the eminent founder of our religion, but He was not pre-existent, nor was He born of the Virgin Mary or raised bodily from the grave.

Under the skillful hands of Abraham Kuenen (1828-1891), the other renowned Leiden father of Dutch Modernism, the entire Old Testament was reconstructed. In his book *The Religion of Israel,* he followed the Pentateuch criticism of the German scholar Graf and placed the supposed sources of the Torah in the following order: Jahwist, Elohist, Deuteronomist, and Priestly Code.* Under the influence of evolutionism, he also concluded that the commonly held order of the Old Testament canon could not be maintained, instead, it should not be Law, Writings, Prophets, but rather Prophets, Law, Writings.

The disciples of the Leiden school accepted this criticism as high and undeniable scientific truth and spread it throughout the country. The church suffered tumult and unrest, and an increasing wave of unbelief. Some of the members of this school of thought felt and openly expressed that they could no longer hold their office in the church with a clear conscience.

Allard Pierson, a gifted son of the Réveil, studied at Leiden under Scholten and Kuenen. He became a minister, but after some years he resigned, writing that the Modern theology "raised much unrest" and that it "silenced the prayer on many lips." He further observed that "many have closed the Bible since it appeared" and that it "attacked in cold blood certain

---

* Pentateuch criticism is the criticism of the five books of Moses (the Torah). It is supposed that these books are made up of various written documents (often called "J," "E," "P," and "D") dating from the ninth to the fourth century B.C.

religious conceptions which are, for their confessors, a source of comfort and spiritual life.''[14]

Pierson deplored these developments, but he believed that they were the unavoidable product of the spirit of the time, which could not be stopped. The man who was to be most energetic in fighting against this spirit was another Leiden student—Abraham Kuyper.

Chapter 4

The Young Kuyper

Parental Home and School Years

In his Stone Lectures on Calvinism, Kuyper developed his theory of the "commingling of the blood." He spoke of the various races of Mesopotamia, Greece and Italy, which combined in one nation that dominated the others, and also of the marriages between the dynasties of the Habsburgs, the Bourbons, the Oranges, and the Hohenzollerns, which produced a host of the most remarkable statesmen and heroes. His conclusion was: "History shows that the nations among which Calvinism flourished most widely exhibit in every way this same mingling of races."[1]

Although this conclusion was flattering to the American public to which it was addressed, its scientific value is questionable, to say the least. However, it might well be applied to Kuyper himself: throughout his life he was as Dutch as Dutch could be, and yet he carried in his veins some foreign blood. His father, Jan Frederik Kuyper, was married to Henriette Huber, the daughter of an officer in the Swiss Army. His paternal grandmother hailed from the German-speaking part of Switzerland.

More important than Kuyper's ethnic origins, however, were the spiritual influences in his childhood home. His father was a minister in the Reformed State Church. Although he was touched by the spirit of the Réveil, he was among the conservatives who feared extremes and accepted the given situation.

In his younger years he had been an office clerk in Amsterdam. Since he knew the English language, he had helped an

Amsterdam Anglican minister named Thelwall to translate some English tracts into Dutch. In this way he drew the attention of the Tract Society, won a scholarship to study theology at Leiden, and became a minister.

While he was in Maassluis, his third congregation, his son Abraham was born, on October 29, 1837. Abraham was a happy child in a large family.[2] In his later works he would often stress the value of such family life as the center and model for the health of the church, the state and society.

In 1841, Kuyper's father accepted a call to Middelburg, the capital of the Dutch province of Zeeland. While living there, young "Bram" dreamed of becoming a sailor. He did not go to school during those years, but received instruction from his parents at home. His father was proficient in English, and his mother excelled in French. Kuyper never had difficulty expressing himself in the major modern languages of Europe. He was also fluent in Latin and Greek and even taught Hebrew for some years at the Free University.

Kuyper studied at the gymnasium* in the city of Leiden, where his father became a minister in 1849. He continued his studies in the gymnasium for six years, until 1855. His history teacher was the famous Robert Fruin, the liberal author of many highly regarded works on Dutch history and the promotor of the idea of impartiality in historiography. In Kuyper's writings we find a number of favorable references to Fruin, especially because of Fruin's estimate of Calvinism as one of the main sources of the spiritual power of the people.**

When he graduated from this preparatory school, Kuyper was chosen to deliver the valedictory address, which he did in the German language. His topic was: "Ulfil, der Bischof de Visigothen und seine gothische Bibeldubersetzung" (Ulfila, the Bishop of the West Goths, and His Gothic Translation of the Bible").

Now the time seemed ripe for Kuyper to throw in his lot with the elite of nineteenth-century Dutch scholarship. There

---

* The Dutch and German name used at that time for secondary schools in which students were prepared for university studies.
** When he was Prime Minister, Kuyper said in a speech in the House of Commons: "According to Robert Fruin and our best historians, the Calvinists were the ones who saved our country in the sixteenth century" (J.C. Rullmann, *Kuyper-Bibliographie,* Vol. III, 1946, p. 287).

were serveral important scholars of the university in Leiden. But Kuyper hesitated and postponed his decision, just as he also hesitated to publicly profess his faith.* In 1855 he enrolled "for literature and theology." In his first years he studied mainly literature, and after three years he received his B.A. in classical literature *summa cum laude.*

Then Kuyper started studying theology in earnest, but with deep and troublesome questions: What was the use of it all? What was the use of the church? He had no enthusiasm for a church with sound moral principles but without prophetic fire. Such a church was out of date, an anachronism.

In 1859, Kuyper wrote a paper for N.C. Kist, his church history professor, called: "The Development of Papal Power under Nicholas I." Kuyper's early eagerness to delve into the mine of church history was something he never gave up.

However the interesting part of this paper is Kuyper's *conclusion.* He wrote that all of history, including church history, must be viewed as a mighty process, and that all the moments of the process follow one another with an inner necessity. At the beginning of this process, the church needs an exterior form. At the end all outward form will be superfluous.

Kuyper expected the final stage to dawn soon. He called the church "the temporary organ of religion" which is destined to merge into humanity. As for humanity, it consists of all free citizens of the times. Those free citizens should observe religion in their hearts and act in public life according to moral principles.[3]

These words were written in 1859. In 1860 something significant happened. Kuyper and his fellow students listened to Rauwenhofff, a young professor who had recently arrived. This professor talked about the resurrection of Christ. He admitted that the Bible witnessed to such a resurrection; but he explained that Scripture often uses symbolic language that has deep meaning. Surely no modern man could believe that Christ's body had been raised in actual fact. That would have been contrary to all the laws of nature, and those laws could never be broken.

When the professor came to this conclusion, the students all rose from their seats and applauded. The young Kuyper, then

---

* He finally took this step when he was a theological candidate, shortly before he was declared eligible for a call (see Rullmann, *A. Kuyper*, p. 23).

twenty-three years old, also applauded. This professor was a man after their own heart—a radical who dared to say aloud what others only dared to whisper.

Kuyper was drawn irresistibly along this path. He decided to become a minister after all and attended the lectures of the famous J.H. Scholten. Scholten fascinated him. "One would have to have been his student personally," he wrote after his conversion, "to understand how a personality like his electrifies students."[4]

Slowly but surely Kuyper had lost the faith of his childhood. As he himself put it some years later: "I had lost my traditional faith, which had not taken root in my unconverted heart."[5]

A Turn in the Road

Kuyper was still not satisfied with the church; he was still not satisfied with himself. At this juncture in his life he was confronted with the Groningen theology in a most remarkable way.

The theological faculty of the University of Groningen had offered a prize for the best treatise comparing Calvin's doctrine of the church with the doctrine of John a Lasco. We saw earlier that the Groningen theologians were no special friends of John Calvin. In their opinion, Calvinism was a foreign element that had been foisted upon the spirit of the original Dutch reformation. A leader of the original reformation was John a Lasco, a Pole who had been superintendent of the congregation of Dutch refugees in London from 1550 to 1553. His ideas would have been milder and more practical than those of the reformer of Geneva.

This was the background to the Groningen prize contest. The young Kuyper might have paid no attention to it if it were not for M. De Vries, his beloved professor in Dutch literature, who knew him very well. De Vries said to him: "This is something cut out for you; give it a try."

Kuyper did try, but he soon found that he had undertaken something well nigh impossible. Works by and about Calvin were abundant, but it seemed that the works of a Lasco had disappeared. Kuyper knew of the titles of some sixteen works by a Lasco, but in all the libraries of Europe only three or four of these works could be found.

Kuyper came to the conclusion that he would have to abandon the project. When he went to Prof. De Vries to tell him he was giving up, this good friend encouraged him to carry on a little longer. He also referred Kuyper to the library of his father, an old minister in Haarlem who possessed a unique collection of historical books.

Kuyper made the trip to Haarlem, again in vain, as it appeared, for no books of a Lasco could be found. But old Rev. De Vries, who could not remember exactly which books he did and did not possess, told Kuyper to come back in a week. Kuyper did so, without much hope. When he arrived a week later, he was shown a collection of books by a Lasco that left him dumbfounded. Later he spoke of this experience in the following words:

> There, as by a miracle of God, I saw a collection of Lasciana richer than any library in Europe possessed or possesses. And I found that treasure, which was the "to be or not to be" for the (Groningen) contest, at the home of a man to whom I had been referred by a faithful friend who had no definite knowledge of this hidden treasure. Yes, only a week before, the owner of that treasure had only superficially remembered the name of a Lasco and could not tell me whether something by this Polish reformer could be found among his precious books. In all seriousness, a man who wants to know what it means to encounter a miracle of God on his path must meet with such a surprise in his struggle for life. I say this now with an infinitely deeper feeling of grateful adoration, but even then it moved my heart in such a mighty way that I renewed my prayer of thanksgiving, which I had neglected for a long time. I could not deny that it was not an old wives' tale to speak of "the finger of God."[6]

This was a moving personal experience for Kuyper. Later in his life he would often speak about the "living God." At *this* moment he felt the presence of that God and began to pray again. He was not yet converted to Christ, but he had become one of those "seekers" who possess the promise that they will indeed find.

He now studied the works of Calvin and a Lasco almost day and night.* In impeccable Latin he wrote his treatise and sent it to Groningen at the end of the year 1860, where it was awarded the highest honors: Kuyper won the prize, the gold medal.

Two years later he published this treatise, with some minor additions and corrections, as his doctoral thesis.[7] As we study the thesis today, we see what a brilliant young theologian Kuyper was, even then. And we also see that in spite of the historical objectivity of which the Leiden school was so proud, he was not unprejudiced. He pictured Calvin as the strict disciplinarian, and a Lasco as much more of an "evangelical." (The followers of the Groningen school called themselves "evangelicals.") Calvin he depicted as the rigid dogmatician, and a Lasco as a much more flexible man who emphasized the practice of the Christian life.

This was grist for the mill of the Groningen theologians, but it was not true to fact.[8] No one could say that Kuyper had tampered with the facts, but he had certainly selected them in accordance with the deepest sentiments of his heart.

His heart had begun to resent the intellectualistic, cold, negative modern theology. It was the trend of the time to advance from the halfway house of the Groningen theology to radical Leiden. Kuyper, however, had gone in the opposite direction: he had moved from Modernism toward the so-called evangelical Groningers. He would soon find that the Groningen theology would not satisfy the deepest needs of his heart, and would eventually become a disciple of the very theologian he had learned to read with a critical eye—John Calvin.

Here we pause for a moment to reflect on the marvelous ways of God. Although the hand of God is present everywhere in history and He reigns over all events, it is a hazardous thing to try to pinpoint that hand. We walk by faith—not by sight. But as we study the history of the Dutch churches in the nineteenth century, we find that Kuyper stands out as a man called by God, a reformer of the church and a battler for the honor of God in all areas of life. How marvelous it is to see how God prepared him for this task! In his own flesh and blood Kuyper knew and experienced the various theological systems that he would later

---

* Kuyper customarily did not go to bed until two o'clock in the morning (Rullmann, *Kuyper*, p. 12).

have to combat. The apostle Paul had been a Pharisee and exactly for that reason could become the great defender of God's free grace against all Jewish legalism. Kuyper had been influenced by Modernism, by the halfway Groningen theology, and later by the ethical theology. In all of this, there was the hand of God, who wanted him to be a man of his time who could lead His people on the way of the Word and the Word alone.

In the meantime Kuyper fell ill of total exhaustion. For ten months he could do nothing more than sit with a book in his hand without reading it. As he was beginning to recover, he read a certain book that made a deep impression on him—a very popular novel by Charlotte M. Yonge entitled *The Heir of Redclyffe.*

In this book two characters stand out—a humble, self-denying young man and an arrogant, proud young man. The first seems to be the loser, and the second the winner. But then comes a moment when the tables are turned. The biblical truth that "God opposes the proud but gives grace to the humble" takes on new meaning in this story. When Kuyper read the dramatic description of the culminating scene in the novel, he felt almost personally involved. Later he wrote: "What I lived through in my soul at that moment I was to understand fully only later. Yet from that hour, after that moment, I scorned what I had formerly esteemed and sought out what I had once dared to despise."[9]

Another element in the book also made an unforgettable impression upon him: the Church of England was pictured as a *mother* who comforts her children through the beautiful words of the liturgy and the dignity of the sacraments. "From then on," Kuyper wrote later, "the preference for established forms, the high appreciation of the sacrament and the esteem for liturgy was rooted in my heart, and they still always make me thirst, with all the thirst of my soul, for such a sanctified church in which my heart . . . can find peace."[10]

Would he find the peace he yearned for? He recovered from his ailment and became eligible for a call. After marrying Johanna Hendrika Schaay, he entered the parsonage of the village of Beesd in the Betuwe.

Chapter 5

Conversion in the Parsonage

Pastor Kuyper

The congregation of Beesd welcomed its new minister with high expectations. He had already preached there on Good Friday of 1863, choosing as his text: "And he bowed his head and gave up his spirit" (John 19:30). His sermon was eloquent that day, just as all his sermons would be. His deep, dark eyes had glowed with enthusiasm. The audience was moved.

In later years Kuyper became ashamed of that Good Friday sermon, because the content was so poor. And he was also ashamed of his inaugural sermon, which he delivered on August 9, 1863, on I John 1:7: "If we walk in the light, as he is in the light, we have fellowship with one another." In the preface to an edition of his selected sermons published in 1913 he wrote that he had not included this inaugural sermon because "when I read it again I saw that the crisis of my faith which I was experiencing at that time had just then started."[1]

He was groping for light from week to week and from sermon to sermon. It was not by chance that he chose these words from the Lord's Prayer for the text of his farewell sermon when his four years of service in Beesd were over: "Forgive us our debts as we forgive our debtors." In this sermon he exclaimed: "I feel now the accusation of my own conscience, that I dared to take office in your midst without having been converted with all my heart to the Gospel, which meant that I made you share, to a certain extent, the vacillations in my own convictions." He also asked: "You, who love me, kneel with me now and pray with me and for me, that the Lord may forgive my debt."[2]

"You, who love me," he had said. There is no doubt that he was indeed a beloved pastor. Most of the members of his congregation were conservatives of the sort described in the first chapter. After he began to preach Jesus Christ and Him crucified in an increasingly powerful way, some of his flock turned against him and showed that they hated him, but others loved him deeply.[3]

Kuyper was their pastor in good times and bad times, as we can see from this excerpt from a letter written by Prof. M. de Vries, Kuyper's beloved teacher: "Congratulations, dear friend, that you with your dear wife and child have been spared in that horrible epidemic, while yet being rightly convinced that you have done your duty as pastor of your congregation and have not shirked the danger."[4] A smallpox epidemic had broken out in Beesd, during which Kuyper had faithfully tended the flock.

Scholarly achievement

In the meantime he continued his historical studies. He had set up a program for himself: he wanted to edit the works (opera) of a Lasco, write a biography of the Polish reformer, and, in conjunction with other specialists, write a history of the Reformation in The Netherlands.

He relied on his iron will, often working until four o'clock in the morning, when his wife insisted that he stop. With much energy and ingenuity, he acquired almost all the available works and letters of the Polish reformer. Once he drew on the help of Bismarck, the Prussian prime minister, and another time he was assisted by the Dutch archivist Groen van Prinsterer.

In 1866 the *Opera* of Johannes a Lasco as edited by Abraham Kuyper were published. Immediately they earned Kuyper a continent-wide reputation. This edition, with its Latin introduction, was a model of historical research. Kuyper was warmly congratulated by Robert Fruin, the dean of the Dutch historians, and also by Eduard Reusz, the co-editor of Calvin's *Opera*.

If Kuyper had followed through with his program, he would have become the first-ranking Dutch church historian of his time. But another program lay in store for him: he was destined not to write about a past Reformation period but to undertake the reformation of the church in his own lifetime.

Contact with the Common Man

In his farewell sermon, Kuyper pointed out that he felt singularly attracted to the common man in the common pew.[5] Later he would often speak of the "little fellows" (*kleine luyden*) of the time of the Reformation, who had persevered when many other people with great names had not persevered. These "little fellows" were unknown soldiers in the Kingdom of God.

When he came to Beesd, he was warned against some of them, who were known as the "malcontents." He was told that they were always critical and that no good purpose would be served by visiting them. But the young shepherd wanted to know all the sheep in his flock. Therefore he also visited these critical people. It turned out that they were stubborn, old-fashioned Calvinists.

They did not receive Kuyper with open arms. They did not trust him because he came from the modern Leiden school. They detected traces of Modernism in almost all of his early sermons. Yet they did not hide their suspicions; they discussed them with him when he visited them.

One of them was Pietje Baltus, thirty years old, the unmarried daughter of a miller. At his first visit she refused to shake hands with him and relented only when he insisted. She would shake his hand not as her minister but only as a fellow human being. Kuyper found out that this unfriendly attitude was not the result of discourtesy or pure negativism but of deeply rooted conviction that dated back to original Calvinism. He came back and visited her again, because he wanted to hear and learn more.

What was the result of Kuyper's contact with the "malcontents"? In his own words:

> I did not set myself against them, and I still thank my God that I made the choice I did. Their unwavering persistence has been a blessing for my heart, the rise of the morning star in my life. In their simple language, they brought me to that absolute conviction in which alone my soul can find rest—the adoration and exaltation of a God who works all things, both to do and to will, according to his good pleasure.[6]

Kuyper took the side of the "common members" of the church with a brochure he published in 1867 under the title *What Must We Do?* He was writing about the main problem of that year in the Dutch Reformed Church: Should we have some sort of Christian democracy in the church or not?

Since 1816, the church had been ruled in an aristocratic way. The members of the synod were appointed by the king; the members of the boards of the provincial and classical board meetings were also government-appointed. Not even the consistory members were elected by the congregations; when vacancies arose, the consistories filled them themselves.

But things were beginning to change. In 1848 revolutions raged throughout Europe. In The Netherlands, too, the cry went up for *more democracy*. In 1852 the Dutch government issued a royal decree which recognized the right of the local churches to appoint elders and deacons and to call ministers.

This decision was finally implemented by the Reformed synod of 1867. The synod decided that either "voters" or "electoral committees" would elect office-bearers and call ministers.

Democracy in the church! There were quite a number of church members who did not know what to do, for they were convinced that the church is to be Christocratic, not democratic. They knew that the old Dort church order allowed for some cooperation on the part of the congregation, but only under the direction of the consistory.[7] Could they accept and implement the synodical decision with good conscience?

In his brochure Kuyper answered this question with a yes. He pointed out that the reorganization of 1816 had created exceptional circumstances in the church, and that there was now an opportunity to correct the situation. There is a difference between false and proper democracy, he argued. He showed his progressive ideas by pleading for voting rights for female members of the church.

The brochure was very well received and favorably reviewed. And in the Dutch church, the effect of the votes cast by the common people was startling. Many liberal consistories turned orthodox. The large city of Amsterdam, which for years had been a bulwark of Modernism, slowly became a center of church renewal. This city was to become Kuyper's headquarters.

Chapter 6

Disturber of the Peace

Kuyper in Utrecht

The consistory of the Dutch Reformed congregation in Utrecht that called Kuyper in 1867 was orthodox. All ten of his colleagues were orthodox. However, Kuyper found himself isolated after a while. His colleagues whispered that he was a fanatic. Some former friends (especially Prof. N. Beets and Dr. J.J. van Toorenenbergen) turned their backs on him. Most of the consistory members, however, continued to support his views.

What had happened? The church of Utrecht was involved in two conflicts in those days. The first one had to do with the *baptism formula*, and the second with the question of *church visiting*.

In all truly Christian churches, the formula for the baptism was and is: "I baptize you into the name of the Father, and of the Son, and of the Holy Spirit." During the course of the nineteenth century, however, more and more ministers in the Dutch Reformed Church could no longer believe in the Trinity. Some of these ministers began to change the baptism formula. One baptized "unto faith, hope and love," another "unto initiation in Christianity," and a third "in the name of Father, Son and humanity sanctified in Christ."[1]

Protests were voiced, but Synod did not act. Synod wanted a single national church with complete freedom of doctrine—even the freedom to deny the essentials of the Christian faith.

Members of the Utrecht consistory felt very uneasy about this situation. It took the courage and leadership of their youngest minister, Abraham Kuyper, to lead them to the decision in 1868 that "in this congregation no other baptism will be recognized than baptism administered in the name of the Father, and of the Son, and of the Holy Spirit." The consistory also decided that guest preachers would not be allowed to administer the sacrament of baptism unless they first promised to use the words ordained by Christ, and that there should be an inquiry into the validity of the baptism certificates presented by new members.

This represented public opposition to Synod's laxity. Even more important was the next step: the Utrecht consistory invited all the other consistories in the country to unite with it in forming an association of consistories dedicated to reaffirming the trinitarian baptismal formula. The Utrecht consistory received positive responses from 143 other consistories. This was the beginning of an organization of local consistories that would resist the power of Synod. Kuyper and the Utrecht consistory dared to go even further. This became evident in the conflict concerning church visiting.

Church Visiting in Utrecht in 1868

What is meant by the term *church visiting*? It refers to an old Reformed practice defined in article 44 of the Dort church order. On an annual basis, two of the most experienced ministers in a classis are to visit the local churches to find out whether the ministers and the consistory are faithfully performing all the duties of their office, adhering to sound doctrine, and observing all that the church order requires. The main concern in these official visits is to investigate the spiritual condition of the congregation and the doctrinal soundness of the office-bearers.

This fine old custom had become a farce in the nineteenth century. Synod tolerated completely opposite and sometimes even outrageous opinions in the church; how, then, could men who came in its name ask any penetrating questions about spiritual life and soundness of doctrine? Did they have any standards to apply? Was there really such a thing as the doctrine of the Dutch Reformed Church?

Already in 1867, about half a year before Kuyper came to Utrecht, the consistory there had decided not to answer the church visitation question about the doctrine of the office-bearers. In 1868 a motion made by Utrecht's youngest minister was passed by the consistory: no longer would any of the church visitation questions be answered, for "they are asked in the name of a Synod with which, as far as its present dignitaries are concerned, consistory has no communion of faith and confession." This was a very radical position, and it might have triggered an explosion. It could have caused the deposition of Kuyper and his fellow office-bearers. But Synod hesitated, and the great conflict did not come until two decades later.

Kuyper explained and defended the position of the Utrecht consistory in his brochure *Church Visiting in Utrecht in 1868.* In this rather emotional publication, he sketched the situation in the Dutch Reformed Church and indicted the Synod in scathing terms. His criticism was comparable to the criticism being leveled against the Danish state church at about the same time by Sören Kierkegaard.[2]

Kuyper pointed to dishonesty in the church in the areas of baptism, the celebration of the Lord's Supper, the public profession of faith, and the examination of candidates for the ministry. Then he continued:

> Lo, a young man does his utmost, with the passion of a renegade and the shallowness of a skeptic, to demonstrate all the negations that can substantiate how he has turned away absolutely from the life of the church. (These facts can be proved.) He gets a hearing. The examination is finished. He absents himself for a while, and is admitted again. And now, not a word of warning; no attempt to make him aware of the conflict between his conviction and the office he seeks; no hint in the direction of the impossibility of signing the form of subscription with a clear conscience. He is handed a book in which he writes his signature beside other signatures, and with that signing something comparable to an oath in the church is given. Before God, I ask each one who still believes in human honesty: Is this not a comedy? Is it not a lie? Is it not intensely immoral to allow a person to start such a career with such an obvious weakening of his moral feelings?

Kuyper also pointed to the lack of discipline with respect to the membership at large and exclaimed:

Nothing is too unholy to be tolerated; nothing is too immoral to be connived at. And *this* is the reality: the brothels and prisons are populated for the most part by recognized brothers and sisters of the church. Members of the church are racketing and rowdying at night in the streets. Members of the church frequent taverns and pubs where they kill their own souls and the happiness of their families. Members of the church keep their mistresses and have their bastards . . . And on the certificates of membership you can read: Sound in doctrine and life.

In this brochure Kuyper appealed for action. He pointed to the example of the Utrecht consistory which had taken the action of refusing to answer the questions of the church visitors.

The effect of this resolute attitude was twofold. In the first place, Synod backed down. The hour for a real confrontation had not yet come. In 1870 Synod declared that church visiting in its written form was only a statistical procedure intended to get some information on the outward situation of the church. In the second place, ministers and common members began to discuss the issues. Much was written both in favor of Kuyper and against him. Some of his friends warned him not to go to extremes; others began to look to him as the coming "judge of Israel."

Meeting with Groen van Prinsterer

On the evening of May 18, 1869, in one of the rooms of the cathedral church (*Domkerk*) in Utrecht, Kuyper met Groen van Prinsterer, the leader of the orthodox Reformed Christians in the Dutch house of commons. This meeting was so important to him that he mentioned this date in a speech more than twenty-five years later, telling his audience that it was on that evening that he met for the first time "the man who by his first glance, by his first word, immediately moved and impressed him so powerfully that from that moment on he became his fellow worker—and even more, his spiritual son."[3]

Despite the fact that Groen had many friends, he was lonely. He had many friends among the men of the Dutch Réveil. He was highly respected by the refined theologians of the Ethical school. Yet the Ethicals were precisely the ones who thwarted him. In 1871, in a letter to Kuyper, he talked about "the indirect criticism of de la Saussaye and Beets, which had greatly hurt his political career."[4] These pious men lived in deadly fear of Groen's consistent Calvinism* and often left him in the lurch.

Now Groen met and heard Kuyper. He thanked God for the meeting. Three years later he wrote about "our beloved and gifted friend, Dr. Kuyper."[5]

What brought them together in 1869? They were involved in the same struggle—the struggle for free Christian schools. When the general meeting of the Association for Christian National Schools was held, Kuyper delivered the opening speech. Groen was present as the honorary president of the Association.

Moreover, both men favored some sort of Christian nationalism—not a secular nationalism that declares, "My country, right or wrong," but a Christian nationalism. On the front page of Groen's textbook on national history, are the words: "We will tell the glorious deeds of the LORD . . . that the next generation might know them . . . so that they should set their hope in God." (Psalm 78).

In his speech "An Appeal to the Conscience of the People," Kuyper called to mind the Christian and Reformed past of the Dutch people. He spoke of the freedom of conscience that had always marked the Dutch and pleaded the cause of those parents who desired Christian instruction for their children but could not afford it. On this occasion, too, he spoke up on behalf of the "common man":

> I myself am also a father, and I am inclined to say that my fatherly heart would suffer and my conscience be hurt if I were forced to have my two sons, who were given to me by God, instructed in a way which . . . I consider to be detrimental to them and which I abhor. But in fact I am not forced to do so. I can even instruct them myself if I cannot find a fitting school. The rich man is not forced either . . . but the common man, the poor man—he is the one I want to speak up for . . . He is either forced to leave his child uneducated or to have him instructed in a way in which, in his opinion, the one thing that is needful is lacking.[6]

---

* Groen often called himself a Calvinist (issu de Calvin), but he declared that the doctrine of predestination was no shibboleth (J.C. Rullmann, *Strijd voor kerkherstel*, p. 66).

From then on Kuyper and Groen were friends. Kuyper became the indefatigable champion of the Christian school movement and lived long enough to witness (in the last year of his life) the complete legal equalization of Christian and public instruction. At that meeting of 1869, however, some of his former friends turned their backs on him (and also on Groen).

Both men wanted consistency; they wanted to call a spade a spade. Therefore they denied that the public school (from which prayer and Bible reading had been removed) could be called a Christian school any longer. Kuyper and Groen did not want to cover up the hard facts. But the men of the middle, the halfway theologians, completely disagreed: there were still so many good things to be said about the beloved institution of the public school.

Then Kuyper asked some of them to cooperate with him in writing a book on biblical topics for the interested church members of those days. Kuyper insisted on agreement on one point: that the Bible is the Word of God. When he made this his condition, his former friends declined to participate, one after another.

Was Kuyper a hard, intolerant, intractable man? No one who heard him address the children in a Sunday school class in the fishing village of Katwijk would have suspected that he was. He talked to the children about the angels in heaven. He told them that the angels are on the lookout for the coming in of men, just as the fishermen's wives on the beach watch for the boats to come home.[7] Kuyper's pastoral sensitivity was demonstrated even more convincingly after he accepted a call to Amsterdam in 1870.

In Amsterdam (1870-1874)

In a play on words, Amsterdam (formerly spelled Amstelredam) was called "Mater Salem," mother of peace. Since the days of the Reformation, the church in Amsterdam had been influential and outspoken in its orthodoxy. During the nineteenth century, however, the liberal spirit of the time had found its way into the meetings of the consistory. Since the man in the pew had no voting rights, one modern minister after the other was called. But this situation changed drastically after the synodical decision of 1867 that introduced "democracy" into the church. Within a couple of years, there was a soundly orthodox majority in the consistory. As a result, Kuyper was called to the capital city in 1870.

Both his farewell sermon in Utrecht and his inaugural sermon in Amsterdam focused on the problem of the church. The farewell sermon was entitled "Conservatism and Orthodoxy," while the first Amsterdam sermon was called "Rooted and Grounded." In "Conservatism and Orthodoxy," Kuyper pleaded for a *true* conservatism, as opposed to a *false* conservatism. False conservatism wants to conserve things as they are, whereas true conservatism wants to preserve the treasures of Jesus Christ. More important was the sermon "Rooted and Grounded," to which Kuyper added the subtitle "The Church as Organism and as Institution."*

From then on, Kuyper would often work with the distinction between organism and institution. This distinction had polemical overtones: the Ethicals put too much emphasis on the elusive idea of an organism, while the conservatives overemphasized the fixed idea of an institution. Kuyper wanted a balanced combination of the two.

In his view, "rooted" meant that the church has its own organic life, not produced or sustained by human power, and not limited to any place or confined to any area. "Grounded" meant that there are still human church-builders, that the church manifests method and order, and that men are responsible for the structure of the church. Kuyper stressed the responsibility of the members of the church. "We must rebuild or move out," he declared. "Our church must again become not only Christian, not only Protestant, but Reformed."[8]

A host of activities was waiting for him in Amsterdam. He was a beloved preacher, pastor, catechist, leader, and author. He preached the whole counsel of God. His second sermon was entitled "The Comfort of Eternal Election." No one had preached on this topic for years in Amsterdam. The situation there was so bad that one of his colleagues immediately delivered

---

* The text was Ephesians 3:17: ". . . that you, being rooted and grounded in love, may have power to comprehend with all the saints what is the breadth and length and height and depth . . ."

a counter-sermon in which he declared: "Cursed is the man who denies that Christ died for all."[9]

Kuyper touched the hearts of the common Reformed people who crowded into the church whenever he preached. He was a master of the art of preaching—not as an exercise in eloquence but as a matter of life and death. When he became a professor, this was the advice he gave his students about preaching:

> You will become preachers, and every week you will find your text. But after you have found it and studied its exegesis, you are not yet sufficiently prepared for making your sermon. You should sit down and meditate in your heart on that text. In doing so you will hear some voices raising objections, because your heart is a sinner's heart that objects to the Word of God. You hold on and listen to all those objections. And then you should conquer all of them in the strength of the Holy Spirit because you have made yourself captive to the Word of God. Only then should you start making your sermon.[10]

Kuyper preached with his head, but he also preached with his heart. A liberal reporter once described what was a strange phenomenon for that time: masses of people coming to hear a minister and taking their places in the church a full two hours before the service started:

> What is the cause of this extraordinary success? In the first place, the theology of which Dr. Kuyper is one of the principal spokesmen. This theology is prevalent in the Amsterdam congregation and is supported by members of the working class. Furthermore, we must point to the remarkable eloquence that impresses all those who hear him, even if they differ in opinion. But the main thing is the fact that Dr. Kuyper knows how to strike the right note, a note that finds an echo of sympathy in the hearts of those who are less privileged, the workers whose cares he shares, whose emotional life carries weight to him, whose well-being is his concern.[11]

Kuyper taught many catechism classes and organized a large class of confessing members. His special care went out to the orphans of the church, who were lodged in a Reformed orphanage. When Kuyper arrived in Amsterdam, they were being instructed by Dr. van Gorkom, the most liberal minister in the city.

Displeased with this situation, Kuyper organized catechism classes for some of the orphans in his own house. After Van

Gorkom's retirement, all the catechism classes for the orphanage were assigned to Kuyper but Van Gorkom declared that his people were ready to go on meeting with him. And in fact, in their answers and written work, his pupils freely criticized the confession of the church. At Kuyper's request the consistory now ruled that the orphans would be free to choose the minister they preferred. Many opted for another teacher, but all who stayed with Kuyper confessed their faith in due time. Thanks to the efforts of Kuyper, the entire orphanage was brought under orthodox leadership.

This was a very important note in Kuyper's life. He was a great leader, but one of his greatest achievements lay in the time and energy he devoted to orphans, children who are cared for by the Lord Himself in a special way, according to Scripture.

A Declaration of War

In 1872 Kuyper wrote his brilliant pamphlet, *The Offense of the Seventeen Elders*. Who were those seventeen elders, and what crime had they committed? In the eyes of some they had neglected their duty; in the eyes of others they had performed their duty. What were the facts?

After the introduction of free elections in 1867, the Amsterdam consistory had been transformed from a liberal body into an orthodox Reformed body. But when an elder registered some form of protest against Modernism in the pulpit, his protest fell on deaf ears. In 1869 the consistory officially censured all preaching that contained a denial or criticism of the miracles of the Bible, but that decision sounded like a voice in the wilderness.

These things changed, however, after Kuyper's arrival in 1870. In 1871 a member of the Amsterdam church sent a letter to the consistory in which he protested against an Easter sermon of Rev. P.H. Hugenholtz which denied the bodily resurrection of Christ. The letter requested that this minister be deposed from office. In accordance with the rules, the consistory passed this request on to the classical board, but the board turned the request down because "the fact of the resurrection of the Lord belongs to those doctrines on which the official rules of the church have not unambiguously expressed themselves."[12]

Deeply disappointed by this decision, seventeen elders discussed the situation together and resolved to take a common stand. By letter, they informed the congregation of their stand: from then on, they would refuse to be present whenever a Modernist minister was preaching or administering the sacraments. This was in effect a declaration of quiet revolution. The elders, of course, set an example to the members of the congregation, suggesting that they no longer attend worship services conducted by the Modernists or recognize them in their office.

This kind of "Reformed intolerance" became the talk of the city. The consistory received a letter signed by over 1000 male members of the church and supported by 245 female members in which the "offense of the seventeen elders" was sharply denounced. Kuyper was assigned the task of replying to this protest.

In short order he wrote a book which included many extracts from the earlier sessions of the Amsterdam consistory. It was a well-documented piece of work which demonstrated that the period of liberal dominance in the consistory had been marked by great intolerance, and also that the consistory meetings during the liberal era had been characterized by incredible banality. Kuyper quoted from the minutes: "After that nothing more to eat and drink was found, and the meeting was closed with a prayer of thanksgiving."

What the seventeen elders had done was not intolerance or an infringement on freedom of conscience but only an effort to defend the character of the church against those who opposed historic Christianity. After this incident Kuyper began to organize the members of the consistory who favored a reformation of the church. At times they met separately and took for themselves the name "Consultation" (*Beraad*).

Confession

In order to defend his action of organizing a special circle of elders, Kuyper wrote one of his finest booklets. He composed it in the form of a confidential letter to one of his friends, the Amsterdam elder Vander Linden. He called this work his "Confession" (*Confidentie*); in it he opened the inner recesses of his heart. As the words poured forth, he told the story of his own conversion.

During the spiritual process that led to his conversion, Kuyper had received the vision of a true church. In this confessional work he told his readers about that kind of church: it should be Reformed, democratic, free, and better organized as far as doctrine, worship and love are concerned.

In the first place, it should be *Reformed*. He pointed to the extreme individualism of the church he knew. Every professor had his own system and his own disciples. In Groningen it was Hofstede de Groot, in Leiden, Scholten, and among the Ethicals, Chantepie de la Saussaye. Such a situation was very unhealthy. Kuyper called it spiritual tyranny and wrote:

> You should not belong to Cephas, Paul or Apollos . . . Be Reformed; honor again that old coat of arms of your spiritual family. Stop trying to be different from (the confession of) your church.

In the same breath he warned against a mere traditionalism and emphasized the old motto "Ecclesia Reformata, quia semper reformanda" (A Reformed church because we never stop reforming).

A Reformed church was Kuyper's ideal, then, but also a *democratic* church. Kuyper foresaw a future of increasing political democracy, which would also affect the church. The Réveil, in spite of all its good qualities, had been very aristocratic. Kuyper pointed out that Jesus had been surrounded by men from the laboring classes and had looked after the multitudes of Israel. And now, Kuyper wrote, the church would be lost without the faithfulness of the common man.

He also pleaded for a *free* church, in contrast to an established church. There was something dreadfully wrong with the church if all the citizens of a country were automatically included on its membership rolls. There was certainly something amiss with the church of Amsterdam with its 137,000 members. "How many members are really involved in the church? Not a sixth of them attend the houses of prayer. Not a tenth attend the catechism lessons. Most of them are abandoned to their own apathy by the church."

Finally, he pleaded for a *better-organized* church with respect to doctrine, worship, and love. Doctrine should not vary with the individual opinions of the ministers; there should be one doctrine for the one church. This did not mean that the confessions of the church could never be changed; Kuyper did express the wish for a new confession in his own time. Yet he cautioned that

> no one should set up something of his own, individually, but everyone should confess his faith with others, in the historical line, with the Confession of our fathers. But if possible, that Confession should be expressed more clearly, and argued more clearly with Scriptural arguments, and maintained more sharply against present-day heresies, which would be more helpful for our present generation.

When it came to the *worship services,* Kuyper certainly wanted the full counsel of God to be preached—but not only that. In addition to services built around preaching, he also wanted to see other services instituted. He wrote: "Let there also be short, simple liturgical services in which each member, even the children, can participate—services in which the Word of God is read, in which thanksgivings and prayers are offered, in which there is singing and jubilation, with a short exhortation to conclude it all."

And he pleaded for a new organization of the service of *love.* The church should really be like a mother. The office-bearers should be prepared to help the members in all their spiritual and physical needs. Personal counseling should include care for the aged, for strangers in the church, for the sick, for prisoners, the blind, the deaf, the mute, and the crippled.

This was Kuyper's ideal when he founded his association of elders. It was quite a program, and it would eventually lead to the rupture of 1886. But then for a while, it seemed that his program of church reform was interrupted.

Chapter 7

A Small Note

The Vision

It happened in 1869, while Kuyper was still in Utrecht. He was sitting in his study thinking. Then he scribbled down some words, containing the rough draft of a letter:

> About an outline that will be printed confidentially.
> About education.
> About the social problem. I would propose: more than thus far took place in journalism . . . all facts concerning the social problem should be pointed out. The Daily (newspaper) should not conceal the immense importance, the dangerous proportions and the terrible consequences of this problem. It should show clearly the unmistakable connection between this problem and the principles of revolutionary statecraft. It should open the eyes of the people to a government that on the one hand conjures up a revolution which it will afterward choke in blood, and on the other hand causes social conditions to be so unnatural and forced that a considerable part of the population can hardly live in this way.
> Finally, it should show how only a constitution founded on the law of nature and on the Word of God can take into account the facts of life and can satisfy the needs of life, revealing itself in Christian faith and love.[1]

These words were written as a kind of memorandum on May 14, 1869, two decades after the *Communist Manifesto* of Marx and Engels was published. We know that on October 29 of that year, Kuyper starting writing political articles in the weekly paper *De Heraut* (The Herald).

He must have been pondering the necessity of reaching out to his fellow Christians with respect to educational, social and political problems. He had jotted down the words of the memorandum quoted above under the influence of a vision. It was the vision of a journal, a Christian daily newspaper. It was the vision of an instrument useful for attracting attention and for giving guidance to the hearts of the thousands in Israel who were like sheep without a shepherd. It was the vision not only of a church but of a country with God—a nation of which Christ would be king.

Member of Parliament

Kuyper got his paper. In 1871 he became editor-in-chief of the weekly paper *De Heraut*, and in 1872 of the daily *De Standaard* (The Standard).

So now Kuyper was not only a busy pastor and teacher, he also wrote weekly meditations and daily articles, as pastor, as teacher, and as a leader of the church at large. He had a special style. He was tender in his meditations, while straightforward, to the point, and practical, in his articles. In his repartee he was brilliant, often witty. He worked day and night. The rumor spread that he never slept.

And of course his voice was heard. Thousands of readers looked forward to the appearance of each issue. Twenty-five years later, Dr. Wagenaar, a well-known Dutch minister and church historian, wrote: "I remember, as if it happened yesterday, how joyfully the paper was greeted in a Calvinist family living in a Frisian village, and how I myself, then seventeen years old, devoured its contents and learned the leading articles almost by heart. Oh, how we delighted in that splendid Standard!"[2]

His voice was heard throughout the country. Reformed Christians from all quarters and provinces identified with that voice, for he spoke what they thought in their heart of hearts. His friend Groen van Prinsterer, the leader of the Christian political party (officially known as the Anti-Revolutionary Party) drew the logical conclusion when he urged Kuyper to run for office as a member of the House of Commons.* Groen hoped

---

* I have used the American phrase "run for office," whereas in The Netherlands a candidate does no more than give permission to have his name placed on the ballot.

that Kuyper would be his successor as leader of the party.

Kuyper was elected in 1874, and then he faced a hard decision. The Dutch constitution did not permit a person to be a member of the House of Commons while holding office in the church as a minister. Could Kuyper forsake his ministry, appreciated and blessed as it had been, in order to become a full-time politician?

In the Amsterdam congregation a prayer meeting was called. His deep need for the prayers of the members of the congregation is apparent in a letter he wrote to Groen:

> I have not yet decided. Included a brief confession. I have never made an important decision of this kind without receiving a sign from the Lord. You understand that waiting of the soul, don't you? That fear of acting against His will, of moving away from His path and going away from Him?[3]

We do not know whether Kuyper received his sign, and, if so, what it was. Most likely the sign he awaited was a heartfelt conviction that grew within him after a period of fervent prayer. In any event, Kuyper did arrive at the conviction that he had to serve his King in parliament in order to reach out to the entire nation. He took his seat on March 20, 1874.

"What would this babbler say?"

He was not received with open arms. What was an old-fashioned minister doing among worldly-wise politicians? Didn't he look a bit like a pigeon venturing in among cats? Some members of the House of Commons mockingly called him "Dominee." Certain of the liberals strove to outdo each other in inventing abusive language to be directed against him.[4]

Kuyper was equal to the task, however. With his amazing knowledge of the facts and his often brilliant eloquence, he set forth his undiluted Christian insights into the questions of the day—the social problem, the colonial question, the issue of the free Christian school, and so forth.[5] He was keenly aware of the abuses to which the "laissez faire, laissez aller" system of the liberals had opened the door. He pointed, for example, to the scandal of child labor: "Out in the country, children of seven years of age work 85 or even 87 hours in a six-day work-week.

The evil is so serious that I know there are children of five or six years of age who must literally be shaken up and doused with water so that they can be sent off to the factory."[6]

He pleaded for a special labor law to ensure social justice. Defending this proposal against the objection that it would serve revolutionary purposes, he spoke of Jesus Christ, who had mercy on the multitudes of Israel. Then, addressing the House of Commons, he opened his pocket Bible and read the first verses of James 5, starting with the words: "Come now, you rich, weep and howl for the miseries that are coming upon you." He continued: "If I myself had spoken these words, which in your ears sound radical and revolutionary, you would have objected. But they were written down by an apostle of the Lord. Can anyone, then, confess Christ and not take the side of the laborer when he complains?"[7]

As far as the colonial question was concerned, Kuyper stressed that The Netherlands had a moral obligation toward its colonies. He was as much opposed to economic exploitation as to the opium trade. He wanted to see the Indonesians educated for eventual independence. His progressive Christian ideas were also apparent in the area of education: he wanted *free schools*—free from the interference of both state and church, and operated under parental direction.

All these speeches, however carefully prepared, were essentially improvisations. There was no systematic exposition of Christian political ideas for Kuyper to depend on. He himself eventually filled that gap with a collection of articles written in 1877 and 1878 in *De Standaard*. These articles were published in book form in 1879 under the title *Ons Program* (Our Program). He referred to this book as "a very ephemeral and incomplete sketch."[8] Actually, it was a felicitous summary and readable application of the principal points that marked Christian politics of that time and place.

Not that Kuyper was always right; sometimes he missed the boat. I will give only one example. In *Ons Program* he was right to state that the government in a Christian country should on the one hand glorify the name of God while on the other hand grant complete freedom of religion and conscience.[9] He declared that this was essentially a Reformed point of view and referred, by way of support, to an oration he had delivered in 1874 under the title "Calvinism: The Origin and Safeguard of Our Constitutional Liberties."[10]

Kuyper had been in his element when he delivered this oration—as a historian, as a Reformed Christian, as a witness against the spirit of his time. He had tried to demonstrate that real freedom is not to be found in the principles of the French Revolution, nor had it emerged from this revolution in practice; rather, real freedom was a gift granted by Jesus Christ and was applied most consistently by Calvinism. That freedom was to be found in greatest abundance in the United States. Kuyper quoted the words of the American historian Bancroft: "The fanatic for Calvinism was a fanatic for liberty." Freedom had also been defended by the English Independents in Cromwell's days, and Kuyper viewed those Independents as genuine Calvinists. Freedom had been the inspiration of the Huguenots and of the Dutch resistance fighters against Spain. Such freedom was founded on the principles, if not the practice, of the reformer of Geneva.

Kuyper had made a beautiful speech, and many of his points were well taken. Yet the main point was not tenable. In 1944 the Dutch historian A.A. Van Schelven published some "emendations" on this oration of Kuyper. Van Schelven was also a Calvinist, but he demonstrated irrefutably that Kuyper was wrong in his main thesis. Van Schelven argued: "Generally speaking, (historical) Calvinism has promoted neither the granting of liberty of religion nor the separation of church and state."*

Off the Track

Around 1875, a strange interlude began in Kuyper's life. It was his second year in the House of Commons, and during that year he went to Methodist revival-meetings, and propagated Methodist ideas.

Now, although there have been and perhaps still are some Calvinistic Methodists, just as there are Calvinistic Baptists,

---

* A.A. Van Schelven, *Uit den strijd der geesten* (1944), p. 190. In 1878, Kuyper had himself acknowledged that "the political theory of our fathers was defective" and that they had often acted wrongly, "contrary to their own principles" (*Ons Program*, p. 85).

most Methodists are Arminians who, like John Wesley himself, do not care for Calvin's ideas at all. The doctrine of the covenant is neglected in their circles. The Methodists have a passion for souls, but not for the subjection of all areas of life to Christ. Their main question is: Are you saved? With this question they go from one revival meeting to the next.

How was it possible that Kuyper was fascinated by this revival movement for a while? Let us look at the history.

In 1873 Dwight Moody, the Billy Graham of the nineteenth century, visited England and Scotland with his friend Sankey. Through his eloquence and his obvious sincerity, he made a deep impression on the hearts of thousands. Among the people who were captivated by him was an American businessman named Robert Pearsall Smith, who was originally a Quaker and later became a Presbyterian. Smith was not a member of any church when he heard Moody. He began to organize revival meetings in Oxford in 1874 at which he emphasized holiness of life.

Kuyper heard about these things from friends who visited England. On April 4, 1875, he wrote in *De Standaard* that he appreciated the work of Moody and Sankey, particularly in the materialistic nineteenth century. In his view, Pearsall Smith made a special contribution:

> Moody and Sankey call the multitudes to repentance, while Pearsall Smith calls only those who are already converted. The fact that believers are so often dead, so spiritless, so powerless, bothers him. He believes that there may and will come a change, when believers realize that sanctification is also an essential part of the treasure they have in Christ.

Kuyper agreed with Smith. Together with many other people from The Netherlands, he visited Brighton, England, that year, where Smith had organized a ten-day revival campaign. To Kuyper this was a wonderful experience of the communion of the saints. At one of the meetings, he himself distributed the elements of the Lord's Supper. He declared: "My cup overflows."

After his return to The Netherlands, Kuyper continued to recommend this movement. He spoke highly of a book by Mrs. Pearsall Smith which had been translated into Dutch. In this book we find the following characteristic passage:

> As far as their way of living is concerned, we always see that real Christians give up worldly amusements sooner or later. They don't like reading novels anymore, or the wearing of jewels, but they dress quite simply without any needless adornments. I have observed that they usually stop smoking tobacco and drinking wine and beer, with the exception of what is prescribed for their health.

In these words we sense something of the Methodist spirit that makes a false separation between nature and grace and also tends, generally speaking, toward a certain sort of legalism. Yet Kuyper recommended Mrs. Smith's book and himself undertook a series of articles on Reformed fasting. But then, quite unexpectedly, he stopped.

Two things caused him to fall silent. The first was the behavior of Pearsall Smith, who turned out to be not quite as holy as he pretended. Rumors began to circulate that he had fallen into sin. Moreover, he proclaimed some strange opinions on the basis of his own interpretation of Solomon's Song of Songs. In the second place, Kuyper suffered a collapse at about this time. Once again, he appeared to be completely overworked. For a long time he was unable to publish a single word.

We are now in a better position to understand how Kuyper could be so fascinated by the tenets of Methodism during a certain period of his life. Part of the answer lies in his personal vulnerability at the time: he was weary in body and spirit. We must also bear in mind that he still carried some Romantic, sentimental tendencies in his soul.

To recover his health, Kuyper went to Nice, in the southern part of France. There he also found rest for his troubled soul. He came to confess the total depravity of man, the total grace of God, and the total truth of God's Word. On that basis he devoted himself completely to his Lord.

In 1885 he wrote to his opponent and friend J.H. Gunning: "In the quiet solitude of suffering that I experienced in Nice, my soul was transplanted to the firmness of the firm and energetic religion of our fathers. My heart had indeed yearned for it before, but it was only in Nice that I took a resolute decision."[11]

After his health was restored and he returned to The Netherlands, he wrote a series of beautiful articles on perfectionism in *De Heraut*.[12] Referring frequently to the Reformed confessions, he demonstrated that perfectionism conflicts with sound Reformed doctrine. Perfectionism had been taught first by Pelagius, then by Roman Catholics (especially Jesuits), then by Socinians, Labadists and Quakers. In this part of the study Kuyper showed again that he was an excellent historian, for he went back to the sources as he pointed out principles and their consequences.

A little later he got to the heart of the matter—a mistaken conception of the holiness of God and of the deep corruption resulting from sin. Carefully he discussed the familiar text: "No one born of God commits sin; for God's nature abides in him, and he cannot sin because he is born of God" (I John 3:9).

This text is one of the mainstays of perfectionism. Kuyper pointed out that its absolute language is confusing even to the perfectionists themselves. We do not read that *some* Christians, or only the very advanced Christians or the saintliest of Christians, do not sin: what we read is that *all* Christians—from the smallest to the greatest—are free from sin. If we take this to mean that the commission of a sin proves that a person is not born again, there would be no real Christians in this world.

Kuyper did not want to change the meaning of the text to: "With a few exceptions, a believer does not sin," or: "Generally speaking, a Christian does not commit sins." He insisted on staying with the words of the text and then compared the believer to a tree—a wild tree into which a good branch had been grafted. We find a double life in such a tree—the life of the old branches and fruit and also the new life. In Paul's words: "Now if I do what I do not want, it is no longer I that do it, but sin that dwells in me" (Romans 7:20).

Kuyper's conclusion is that a born-again Christian can speak of himself in a twofold way. When he speaks of his old nature, he declares: "If we say we have not sinned, we make him a liar and his word is not in us" (I John 1:10). When he speaks of his old nature *now*, he declares: "If we say that we have no sin, we deceive ourselves and the truth is not in us" (I John 1:8). But when he speaks of the work of the Spirit of God in his heart, the statement made by Jesus always proves true: "A sound tree cannot bear evil fruit" (Matt. 7:18).

Kuyper concludes: "The unconverted man and the converted man both observe sin in their lives. But this is the dif-

ference: the unconverted man *commits* the sin with his own will
and knowledge, while the converted man *experiences* the sin and
prays against it because he suffers by it and wants to break with
it"[13] (see Romans 7:20). Instructed by his own experience,
Kuyper gave instruction to the Reformed people. Thousands
upon thousands learned once again to spell out the Reformed
first principles.

Chapter 8

A Great Enterprise

Increasing Secularization

Well into the nineteenth century, The Netherlands considered itself a Christian nation, and more specifically a Reformed nation. Magistrates had to be members of the established church, and teachers had to subscribe to the Reformed confessions. Catechism was taught in Christian day schools. Universities were state-controlled, but the professors usually represented the Reformed persuasion of their time.

But as the nineteenth century wore on, all of this began to change. Although the term "Christian" was retained, genuine, undiluted Christianity was removed from public events and statements. Neutrality was the new objective.

In the 1850s a number of public school teachers were dismissed because they read from the Bible or prayed or used the name of Jesus Christ during their lessons. The result was that free Christian schools began to be established throughout the country. Earlier we saw how much Kuyper was interested in those Christian schools and how he defended them.

Things came to a head in 1878 when Kappeyne van de Coppello, the liberal prime minister, introduced a bill which raised the standard for public instruction but which would at the same time make it virtually impossible to establish and maintain free Christian schools because of new high costs. Kuyper wrote about this matter in *De Standaard*: "The law is as liberal as can be. You may certainly have a school with God's Word, if you pay for that school, but—listen well—only after you have paid for your neighbor's school."[1]

73

Kuyper headed a referendum drive. The result was that some 305,102 people (out of a population of four million) and 421 churches signed a petition requesting the king not to sign the bill. But the king, who was a constitutional monarch, signed, and the law went into effect. Even so, a movement had been launched, a movement that would not be stopped until the free school had won the same rights as the public school.

The secularization of public life also had its effect on public higher education. The Constitution of 1848 provided for complete freedom of higher education. This meant that there was to be no interference by the state, the church, society, or the university to restrict any professor in his freedom of thought or expression.

The outcome, as one might expect, was that the spirit of the time came to rule the chairs held by the most gifted professors. This effect was manifested in a clear and deadly way in the life of the young Kuyper, who lost his faith in Leiden's lecture halls. The same thing happened to many other students. The Dutch minister Bronsveld expressed the feelings of many in his poem "Mother's Complaint":

> They have torn him away from me,
>   With all their doubting, so smart,
> My boy whom I have loved so much,
>   Whom I once bore under my heart.

Could the modern theology still call itself Christian? This question was answered when a new law concerning higher education was passed in 1876. The law stated that from then on, the theological departments of the universities would no longer teach systematic and practical theology but would make the "science of religion" their main subject instead. The law recognized that there are a number of religions in the world, of which Christianity is but one though perhaps the highest. It wished to see this fact honored as the theological students were taught about the phenomenon of religion and instructed in the history of religion. Also, because the theological students intended to become ministers, the synod of the established church would be allowed to appoint two professors at each of the three universities. Those professors would then prepare them for their future office.

When this law was drafted and presented to the House of Commons, a number of orthodox Reformed leaders were alarmed. One of the Ethical leaders, Dr. Gunning, who was always highly respected by Kuyper because of his heartfelt piety, proposed in 1875 that a Christian university be established. Kuyper agreed with this proposal and promised to cooperate in the venture. He then tried to organize an association of Christian scholars on a broad basis, but he did not succeed; he ran into opposition from some half-hearted Christians who did not like his radicalism.

At that point Kuyper made a firm decision. Realizing that only the real Calvinists were willing to make the sacrifices necessary in order to stand up for Christ in all areas of life, in 1878 he and his friends founded the Association for Higher Education on the Basis of the Reformed Principles.

In his personal experience and also in his efforts to preserve and restore the Christian character of the nation, Kuyper had found that only undiluted Reformed principles would endure to the end. This was the beginning of the Free University of Amsterdam.

An Act of Faith

The Free University has often been called Kuyper's *act of faith* (*geloofsstuk*). It seemed a grotesque adventure—a quixotic enterprise. What Kuyper had in mind was not a seminary or some sort of Bible college; he wanted a full-fledged university that would teach not only theology but also science, not only literature but also medicine—in short, the entire range of advanced human knowledge.

Where would the manpower come from? Undoubtedly there were Christians who were scientists, but would they be willing to serve in this almost primitive school, with its narrow basis, seemingly far removed from the mainstream of life? And where would the money come from? Undoubtedly some of Kuyper's friends were well off, but the vast majority of his supporters were among the "little people." They were willing to help financially, but were they able?

The closing words of Kuyper's great speech given to open the University gave eloquent expression to the real situation:

> If this enterprise did not depend on the Mighty One of Jacob, how would it be able to make a stand? What we are venturing to do here is to go against and counteract all that is called great; we are going against an age of enormous enchantment. Therefore you may freely despise our persons, our power, and our scientific importance if you feel the need to do so . . .

The Heart of the Matter — I

I have quoted from Kuyper's great inaugural speech of 1880. His title was "Sovereignty in the Distinctive Spheres of Human Life." His main thesis was (1) that God Almighty is solely sovereign over all His creatures, (2) that He turned all power in heaven and on earth over to His Son Jesus Christ, and (3) that the sovereignty of Jesus Christ must be recognized in every distinctive sphere of life.

When the state claims to be sovereign over the church or education or family life or social life, it becomes an idol. When the church does the same and claims to be qualified to rule over kings and princes or to operate businesses or to fight wars, it becomes an idol. In His wisdom, God created several distinctive spheres of life; in His grace He kept and restored them after they were corrupted by sin. They can function properly only by being subject to Jesus, the King of kings.

Let Christ be King! This should be the motto of the statesman, the businessman, and also the man of science. The Free University should therefore be free from the authority of the secular state and also free from the arrogance of secular science. The University should be subject only to the One in whom all the treasures of wisdom and knowledge are hid.

This freedom does not mean having no principles at all, for any science worthy of the name is founded on principles. The University should be free from *wrong* principles and founded on the Word of God—the Word found in Holy Scripture and sealed by the testimony of the Holy Spirit in our hearts.

This was the main concept of Kuyper's inaugural address. Another important address followed a year later.

The Heart of the Matter — II

In 1880 Kuyper had spoken of the Word of God as found in Scripture. What was the relationship between these two terms? Could the Word of God be identified with Scripture, or was Scripture only a time-bound, defective bearer of the Word? This question became crucial when Dr. J.T. De Visser, an able young theologian in the Ethical camp, published his thesis in 1880 entitled "The Demonology of the Old Testament."

The Ethical theologians had always been in favor of a warm personal relationship with God through Jesus Christ, but they were opposed to what they considered the idolatrous worship of the Bible. Therefore they often found themselves at loggerheads with Groen van Prinsterer, and at times they showed their aversion for the activism of Kuyper.

In an article in *The Herald,* Kuyper warned against De Visser's ideas. He wrote:

> De Visser teaches that Genesis 3 is not from Moses; it is not from the time of Moses but from a much later time, from the days of the kings. He teaches that in that supposed time this piece of the Bible was composed not as a description of facts that had really happened but as products of imagination framed by the author's fantasy. The revelation in this respect is only this, that God had roused certain elements of truth in the consciousness of some pious men . . .
>
> Now, we declare as firmly and decidedly as possible that this way of thinking is absolutely modernistic; that it takes the foundation of Scripture away from the faith of the church; and that scholars who foster this opinion (of course, apart from the personal condition of their heart, upon which we cannot and will not pass judgment) should tell the congregation: our scientific point of view with respect to Scripture is contrary to that of the church of all ages, and is essentially the same as that of the Moderns.[3]

Because of this bold language, Kuyper was attacked. He defended himself and elucidated his point of view in an address of 1881 entitled "Present-day Biblical Criticism in its Precarious Tendency for the Congregation of the Living God."

In this oration, which is still very readable,[4] Kuyper first of all explains what theology is. Theology is not the knowledge of the inner life of the Christian soul (Ethical theology) or the science of religion-in-its-evolution (Modernism). It is and remains in the first place knowledge of the self-revealing God; it is *theocentric.* Here Kuyper quotes approvingly the old motto of Thomas Aquinas: "Deo docetur Deum docet ad Deum ducet" ("Taught by God, it teaches about God and leads to God"). True theology suffers when the primary energy of students is devoted to an "Introduction to the Old and New Testaments" and when their main studies are directed at the knowledge of all kinds of literary and historical things instead of at the ways of the living God.

Kuyper continues by emphasizing that the Bible is the Word of God for everyone—for the professor as well as the working man. He then makes a personal confession:

> When I read the sacred Scriptures in private or at the family altar, I am addressed neither by Moses nor by John but by the Lord my God. It is He who narrates to me the origin of all things and the calamitous fall of man. God tells me with silent majesty how He has appointed soul-salvation for our fallen race. I myself hear Him relate the wonders He has wrought for our deliverance; I hear Him tell how, when His people rebelled against Him, He afflicted them in His wrath, and how, when they were chastened, He restored them again in His favor, while they sought the day of the coming of the Son of His love. In the midst of that sacred history I hear the Spirit singing in my spiritual ears as I read the psalms which disclose the depths of my own soul . . .
>
> At length, through the pages of the New Testament, God brings out to me the Expected One, shows me the place where the manger stood, points out to me the tracks of His footsteps, and on Golgotha lets me see how the Son of His unique love, for me, poor doomed one, died the death of the cross . . .
>
> Call this, if you will, an almost childish faith outgrown by your larger wisdom, but I cannot better it. *Such is the Bible to me.* Such it was in bygone ages, and such it is still—the Scripture of the church of the living God.[5]

In speaking about the *inspiration* of the Bible, Kuyper stresses both the *verbal* and *organic* aspects. Verbal: "Scripture is God's Word, both as a whole and in its parts." Organic: ". . . by calling forth the words from man's own consciousness, by employing all those words which were on hand in the spiritual senses of the writer."

The following principles are indispensable to this position:

1. The Holy Spirit can neither lie nor err. "To pretend, for

instance, that in books which one accepts as canonical the Holy Spirit represents myths as history and places before us a *vaticinium ex eventu* (a prophecy written down after it was fulfilled) in a false form of prophecy, is to attribute to the Spirit absurdities that are inconsistent with His integrity."

2. We should listen obediently to what Scripture says *about itself.* "If, then, Christ and His apostles declare that the Scripture of the Old Covenant really is inspired and binding even to the extent of the individual word . . . and if I should reach a conclusion contrary to this (as do the Ethicals), I would thereby have forfeited the right to call myself a theologian."

3. We should not introduce philosophical principles that conflict with the principle of inspiration, e.g. evolution, synergism, humanism, or the relativity of all religions.[6]

Finally, in this oration, Kuyper pointed out that the biblical criticism he was opposing would ultimately lead to unbearable clericalism. "Youthful preachers who scarcely have an elementary knowledge of the original languages often substitute a translation expressing their own ideas, tell us that the original text is hopelessly impaired, that this narration is a myth, and that Daniel was a pious fraud."[7] Kuyper ends with a plea: "Have pity, have mercy, upon those who are deeply hurt, because they are the church of the living God."

When the address was published, some of the Ethical theologians accused Kuyper of being an antiquated defender of a mechanical theory of inspiration. To respond to this criticism, Kuyper wrote some articles in *The Herald* in which he showed that such talk had always been the easy way out: whenever the orthodox Reformed theologians had defended the infallibility of Scripture, they had been accused of talking about robots, mechanical men.* He added that Reformed theology had never propounded a mechanical theory of inspiration but had always pointed out the human factor in the composition of holy Scripture. He quoted from the *Synopsis,* which was the Reformed academic textbook of the post-Dort period:

---

* Kuyper mentioned Herder, the supra-naturalists, the Groningen school, and his teacher Scholten.

Sometimes the Lord inspired and dictated in such a manner that the authors of the Bible wrote down what He had said. At other times the Lord did nothing more than provide help for them and give direction to their spirit, while they themselves acted as thinkers and writers indeed. They certainly were not always passive; rather, they behaved as active persons with the energy of their spirit, as men who had their own ideals, the activity of their own spirit, the forethought and memory and arrangement of their own thoughts, which caused their own way of writing.[8]

It was on this dedication to Scripture—all of Scripture—that the Free University was founded with this foundation, it could recognize the kingship of Christ over the totality of life.

Appendix I:
A Contemporary Evaluation of the Free University

In 1963 Prof. Bernard Ramm of California Baptist College delivered a series of lectures on the Christian college in the twentieth century. In these lectures he gave a prominent place to Abraham Kuyper and his university, calling him "the sacred secular."[9] He could just as well have said that Kuyper accepted the whole world and all the activities of that world as God-given opportunities to glorify God through Jesus Christ.

Ramm set forth two principles. The first of them is that a Christian university is justified by the Christian doctrine of creation. Man was created by God to be the lord of the natural order, to found a society, to create a culture within this society, and to understand creation. This was not the task of one individual man but of humanity as a whole, which is an organic, social and cultural unity. But sin has destroyed the willingness and ability of man to fulfill this task. It has not, however, destroyed the purpose of God: in His special grace, He sends a Savior who renews the heart and life of man. In His common grace, God upholds the entire world and preserves the ordinances of creation.

Ramm showed how Kuyper emphasized the doctrine of common grace: "Common grace is God's grace which so retards sin and so strengthens man's powers that he is able to carry out to some degree of success the original creation purposes of God." Because of common grace, the Christian can appreciate art, culture and education without for a moment denying the effects of sin. The doctrine of common grace enables the Christian to proclaim the goodness of the world without confusing the rule of Christ with the dominion of sin.

Ramm drew the following conclusion:

> A university is the most effective institution devised of men to perpetuate man's cultural life, his scientific life, and his theological life. It is grounded in the doctrine of creation and in the doctrine of common grace. It follows from the doctrine of creation, for it is man's concerted effort to create culture, perpetuate culture, and through science to be the lord and knower of the universe. It follows from the doctrine of common grace, for it is one of those institutions of man created and sustained for the good of the human race. Therefore, only the Christian has the real justification for a university."[10]

Ramm added that a seminary was not enough, in Kuyper's view. Only a complete university can fulfill the needs of the church and the state. Kuyper argued for the inclusion of the five faculties of the Dutch universities of his time, i.e. Theology, Philology and Philosophy, Jurisprudence, Natural Science, and Medicine. Each of these faculties corresponds to a fundamental relationship between man and himself, his culture, or the universe.

Appendix II:
What Are the Reformed Principles?

In the basic formula for the free University, only general Reformed principles of creation and common grace were mentioned, but the Theological Faculty, where students were trained for the ministry, was bound to the confessional standards of the Reformed Church.

As long as all the professors were animated by the same ideals and were Reformed or Calvinistic in their profession, the expression "Reformed principles" seemed clear enough and needed no further explanation. But as soon as one of them objected to Calvinism in some way or did not agree with some of its main tenets, this expression began to look like a fisherman's net full of gaps.

A problem first came up in 1895, when Prof. A.F. De Savornin Lohman, who taught law, was accused in a meeting of the Free University Association of deviating from the Reformed principles. A fact-finding committee was appointed. Conclusions were drawn. The outcome of the story was Lohman's resignation in 1896.

For a number of reasons, this episode was tragic. Kuyper and Lohman were both faithful servants of God, but they could not find a way to each other's heart. It was only shortly before they died that they became completely reconciled again.[11] There were some personal frictions and differences in political insight (Kuyper wanted an extension of the suffrage, but Lohman was opposed). Still, these matters, however influential, were not decisive. What mattered was that many of the common Reformed people did not completely trust Lohman. Although he was treated fairly, it is still not clear whether he really should have been dismissed because of an alleged deviation from the broadly formulated "Reformed principles."

It cannot be denied that there were differences between Kuyper and Lohman. By a long and arduous route, Kuyper had become a full-fledged Calvinist; Lohman was and remained a son of the Réveil. Kuyper was a democrat; Lohman was an aristocrat. Kuyper was a man of the people; Lohman was an individualist. Kuyper himself once explained the difference between their positions by pointing to the difference between *Methodism* and Calvinism. The Réveil position of Lohman was like that of Methodism, which holds that the Christian religion does not influence politics and science directly but promotes moral qualities and honesty. The Calvinist position was that in the Word of God we also find ordinances for political life, for God's sovereignty covers everything.[12] Lohman spoke of Vinet as his spiritual guide and did not want to be called a Calvinist. He did not speak of the Bible as infallible and did not find political principles in the Word of God, as Kuyper did. But no one could have any misgivings about the sincerity of his Christian convictions.

In order to clarify the issue, the professors of the Free University developed eighteen theses in which they explicated the expression "Reformed principles." They started by declaring that the Reformed principles are the principles of Calvinism, in which we find the most consistent worldview developed in the Reformation (thesis 1). They continued by declaring that these principles should not be formulated in a merely negative way but should be stated positively as the governing principles of thought for all of human life (thesis 3). Not only should the ideas of Calvin be defended, but we should try to draw logical consequences from them for our own time (thesis 5). We know Calvinism as explained from Scripture, as explained in the confessions of the Reformed churches (thesis 11), their liturgical forms, church order and dogmatic consensus (thesis 12), and also from the polemics of the original Calvinists against the Roman Catholics, Anabaptists, Socinians, Lutherans, and Arminians (thesis 13). A third source of knowledge is the history of the Reformed churches (thesis 14). Still another source of knowledge is the Calvinistic scientific and aesthetic literature (thesis 15). The study of non-theological subjects should be governed by the Calvinistic confession of creation, of the sovereign reign of God over this world, of the essence of man and the cosmos, of the fall into sin and the distortion of the original creation inside and outside of man, and of the special and common grace of God which controls the present situation (thesis 17).

These theses were rejected by Lohman, who claimed that they overrated historical Calvinism. It can hardly be denied that they were light to the eyes of those who could see, that is, to trained Calvinists. However, they were not formulated in a concise and lucid way which might have helped settle a really controversial case.

Kuyper himself, who must have been primarily responsible for the drafting of these theses, was aware of the difficulty. In 1879 he wrote that he was not in favor of having the professors sign a form of subscription, for experience had borne out that such a step was often a mere formality.[13] Apparently the theses were meant to serve as guidelines for discussion when conflicts arose. Then decisions would have to be made in the existential situations.

Chapter 9

Reformer of the Church

Seventy Years of Exile

In 1886 Kuyper wrote three pamphlets in rapid succession, all of them bearing the same suggestive title—"The Conflict Has Come." In the second one he stated that the Dutch Reformed Church of Amsterdam, of which he was an elder at the time, had experienced seventy years of exile, lasting from 1816 to 1886.[1]

What did he mean by "exile"? In the first place he was referring to the fact that this church had lost its Christian freedom in 1816 when it was annexed by the state. Through his royal decree of that year, King William I had become the lawgiver of the church. In the second place, Kuyper meant that Modernism had entered the church after 1816 and had permeated the pulpits, homes, and hearts of the people. A foreign king had usurped the place of the real King.

Some years earlier Kuyper had described Modernism, to which he himself had once adhered, as *the* heresy, *the* doctrinal error of his time. He had sketched the typical confession of a Modernist:

> I believe in a God who is the Father of all men, and in Jesus—not the Christ but the rabbi of Nazareth. I believe in man who is good by nature and must only press on to become perfect. I believe that sin is only a relative matter, and that forgiveness of sins is therefore only a human invention. I believe in the hope of a better life, and in the salvation of all souls, without judgment.[2]

As we have seen, Kuyper had fought this Modernism tooth and nail in Utrecht and in Amsterdam. After he was elected a member of parliament he had moved to The Hague, but he had returned to Amsterdam in 1879 when he became rector of the Free University. He was also an elder in the church in Amsterdam. There he resumed the battle which he considered to be the most important spiritual battle of the age. He himself called it the "battle in all countries of Europe and America for the *to be or not to be* of the Christian name."[3]

The central issue was the confession of Jesus Christ, and Him crucified. The lines were drawn more clearly because of two synodical decisions, one made in 1880 and the other in 1883. The 1880 decision related to church membership at large, while the 1883 decision had to do with the ministry. Both of them came down to this: modern members had to be accepted without any ado by the local churches and modern candidates had to be admitted to the ministry without any restraints, provided they promised to promote the interests of the Kingdom of God. The church faced the danger of turning into an apartment building, a structure not built on the rock of the confession of Christ, but a structure in which all sorts of opinions could coexist in endless dialogue.

A Reformational Agenda

Every important meeting has an agenda. What the word "agenda" means literally is "what should be done." Kuyper wrote an agenda for the Dutch Reformed Church in his *Tract of the Reformation of the Churches* (1883). This book was published in commemoration of the 400th anniversary of the year of Luther's birth and consisted of lectures Kuyper delivered in 1882 to a circle of consistory members who wanted to discuss the situation of the church.

Just as Luther had reformed the Roman Catholic church of his day, so Kuyper wanted to reform the Dutch Reformed church of his time. In his penetrating study of the essentials of the church, he stressed the primacy of the local congregation with its office-bearers, and the office of all believers as the source of all the special offices in the church. He showed how the church could be corrupted by deformation, using for illustration the situation in the Dutch Reformed churches at the beginning of the seventeenth century, when Arminianism began to prevail in some parts of the country. What had the church members of those days done when they were forced to listen to teachers of error every Sunday?

They did not leave the church or separate from it but instead organized meetings of their own, which they called "dolerende" (complaining or lamenting) churches. These lamenting churches claimed to be a continuation of the original church, with only one change: they had removed the false doctrine and the false office-bearers who had encroached upon the church.[4]

Kuyper wanted the believers of his own time, preferably under the leadership of their consistories, to break with the organization of the church because it tolerated Modernism. They could then declare themselves a free church. Kuyper called this procedure "Doleantie." This term meant that he did not want to champion a secession but a renewal. In other words, he did not brand the Dutch established church a false church, but insisted that it was an unfree church, a church bound by an arbitrary organization.

Kuyper distinguished between (i) true churches, (ii) churches that were more or less deformed, (iii) churches that were totally deformed, and (iv) false churches. In his view there was not yet a totally false church in the absolute sense of the word, not even the Roman Catholic Church. The totally false church will be the future church of satan.[5]

In speaking of the Dutch state church, then, Kuyper chose his words with care. He distinguished between three types of local churches. (i) Quite a number of them, perhaps 500 or 600, were still characterized by a fairly pure ministry of the Word and sacraments. (ii) Other local churches did not possess such ministry any longer but still had a certain number of ministers who prayed for it; hence there was still hope for recovery. (iii) In yet other local churches there was nothing but desecration of the Word and sacraments. In connection with such churches one could only repeat what Scripture says: the candlestick will be removed from its place.

Kuyper advised that the work of reformation should always keep local circumstances in mind. "Lamenting" churches should spring up everywhere. The final goal was a reunion of the "lamenting" churches with the churches of the Secession of 1834.

Lamentations

It was indeed a lamenting Kuyper who preached at a prayer meeting held in Frascati, an Amsterdam meeting hall, on January 11, 1887. He had read Psalm 42, which opens with the touching words: "As a hart longs for flowing streams, so longs my soul for Thee, O God." His text he took especially from the words: "Why are you cast down, O my soul?"

Kuyper preached with the deep feeling of his heart, stressing two essential points. The first was that the name "Reformed" means that God has entrusted some of His most precious jewels to the churches bearing that name—the jewels of giving Him the glory not just for some things, such as the salvation of the soul, but for everything from eternity to eternity. The second point was that the first-class Reformed people in The Netherlands had sinned greatly. They had allowed error to be preached from their pulpits and the name of God to be reviled. Kuyper ended his sermon by quoting from Psalm 130: "Out of the depths I cry to Thee, O LORD!" Then he prayed.

What was the occasion? Many things had happened in the few years since Kuyper had written his reformation agenda. First of all, synod had decided, as mentioned earlier, that the doors of the church must be thrown open as widely as possible to every possible doctrine. Then in that same year, the consistory of Amsterdam had invited all the other church councils to send delegates to a congress to be held in Amsterdam. At that congress it was resolved that no one should be admitted to the ministry of the Word if he did not submit himself wholeheartedly to the Word of God and was therefore willing to sign the confessions.

This conference was in fact the prelude to the *Doleantie,* the movement of local churches who deplored the situation in the Dutch Reformed Church but wished neither to secede from the church nor to obey the directives and rulings of the synod any longer. The center of this movement of local churches was the Amsterdam consistory. The leader was Kuyper, assisted by his friends Rutgers, Lohman, van den Bergh, and others. The movement was launched when the Amsterdam consistory refused to admit to the Lord's Supper some young catechumens who had been instructed by modern preachers and did not confess that they were reconciled with God through the blood of Christ.

It was a long story: the young people who were not admitted by the front door tried to enter by the back door, for they asked for certificates that would enable them to join a neighboring church temporarily. The consistory, however, decided that it would grant such certificates only after they had signed the following declaration:

> The undersigned, who believes in his heart that the doctrine which is contained in the Old and New Testaments and which is taught in this Christian church, is the true and perfect doctrine of salvation, asks for a certificate.

The issue was now perfectly clear: either the doors of the church would be kept open to what the apostle Paul had called every wind of doctrine, or the doors of the church would be closed to unbelievers.

It was small wonder that the higher church authorities now began to take action. As in most such cases, there was maneuvering on both sides. At the beginning of 1886, the majority of the members of the Amsterdam consistory (five ministers, forty-two elders and thirty-three deacons) were suspended from office by the Board of Classis Amsterdam. The suspended office-bearers did not break with the church, however; they appealed to synod. It was in that year that Kuyper wrote his three pamphlets on the theme, "The Conflict Has Come."

There is a remarkable personal comment at the end of the third pamphlet. There Kuyper defended his personal honor against those who claimed that he was the leader of a church revolution—in effect the head of a band of rebels. He wrote:

> I would like to have the privilege of personally answering the question: What does Dr. Kuyper really have in mind? Anyone should know that all that is in me yearns and pants to be delivered from the church struggle with all its bitterness that is so harmful to the soul. In great thankfulness I will bless the hour in which my opponent grants me the hearing of that silent prayer.
>
> I have no time for it. The study of theology demands my total attention to an increasing degree. And if the Lord my God has destined another ten years of life for me, I should like with all my heart and soul to be allowed to publish first my *En-*

cyclopedia, then my *Dogmatics,* and finally, as the conclusion of my life's work, an exposition of one of the books of the Word. I have no higher and further aspirations.[6]

Kuyper did not like and did not want turmoil in the church. Even so, he spoke as he did in Frascati in 1887. He lamented, he prayed, and then he called people to action.

The appeal to synod did no good: seventy-five members of the consistory decided to "shake off the synodical yoke." Kuyper was not an Independent, and he was ready to accept the authority of a *spiritual* synod. But he and his followers did not recognize the authority of the existing synod any longer, they called it a hierarchy.

The congress advised the delegates of the various churches on how to act. But many of the delegates found their course set for them when they arrived back home: they found that their local classical board had suspended them from office simply because they had attended the congress. They then started a local "lamenting" church, and so the *Doleantie* movement spread throughout The Netherlands.

In 1887 there were *Doleantie* churches to be found in all the provinces of The Netherlands, with the exception of Limburg, which was heavily Roman Catholic. It was a time of firm convictions, but also a time of many tears. The rupture embittered many hearts and ran right through many families.

Rejoicings

In 1891 Kuyper found himself presiding over a provisional synod. The synod met in The Hague and was composed of delegates from the newly formed *Doleantie* churches. On the 15th of September, Kuyper, as chairman, delivered a speech which concluded with the words: "Zion of God in The Netherlands, today is the day on which the garment of mourning for our dividedness may be put off, and the wedding garment is being arrayed around your shoulders. Sing, then, to the glory of God, all you servants of the Lord"[7] (Psalm 134).

It was a day of rejoicing. What was the occasion? Delegates from the Secession churches (the churches that had begun to secede from the established church in 1834) were present. A unanimous decision had been made that the Secession churches would join hands with *Doleantie* churches to form one united Reformed church, which would then be known as the Reformed Churches in The Netherlands.

This development was certainly a great gift of God. In this sinful world it is easier to be divisive than to unite. The words "schism," "rupture" and "secession" permeate the vocabulary of church history. When two church communities, each with its own history, unite because each has lost its original moorings and has found itself in conflict with the times, a great deal of statesmanship and self-denial is required; there is nothing automatic about such a union. When two such church communities who both hold firmly to the authority of the Word of God and to the confessional standards unite to become one, it is one of God's little miracles.

Certain small matters can sometimes become almost insurmountable difficulties. Private opinions can cause distrust. What's more, two or three captains on the bridge often make it impossible to sail any further. Difficulties of this sort came along with Abraham Kuyper's personality.

Kuyper was not a quarrelsome man, but neither was he an easy man. He could get along with the lowest of the low and the highest of the high; he certainly was not narrow-minded. But he was used to getting his own way, and he generally found it easy to silence his opponents. Sometimes he created an impression of high-handedness, of not quite being fair to his opponents. It was not without reason that Herman Bavinck, the well-known dogmatician of Kampen, wrote to his friend Dr. Snouk Hurgronje in 1888: "Many among us are a little bit afraid of the supremacy of Dr. Kuyper."[8]

Moreover, some of the ministers in the Secession churches accused Kuyper of hyper-Calvinism, of carrying his logical conclusions too far, and making statements that were not sufficiently warranted by Scripture. They pointed particularly to two areas—predestination and regeneration.

It cannot be denied that Kuyper, after having tried out all the rational and emotional systems of his time, found rest for his mind and heart only in God's eternal counsel concerning human salvation, which was executed in time through the work of Jesus Christ and through the creation of a new heart in the sinner by the power of the Holy Spirit. Kuyper believed in absolute predestination, a position often called supralapsarianism. He also believed in the absolute act of regeneration which precedes the conversion of the sinner and can take place even in the heart of a young child.

He was accused of leaving too little room for the acitivity of man, and of shifting the whole drama of deliverance from time to eternity. It was also said that according to his view, one would have to tell all children of the covenant that they were already born again and did not need to be converted.

These accusations were not well founded. First of all, a number of the great Reformed leaders, such as Beza, Voetius and Gomarus, were supralapsarians, and the Synod of Dort did not condemn this position but permitted it. It should be added that anyone who had read, for example, Kuyper's sermon delivered on the last day of 1871 on the text "Repent, for the kingdom of heaven is at hand," can hardly maintain that he did not call people to conversion or that he failed to spur people to action.

As for the second accusation, Kuyper taught that the rule of the covenant is that we accept our little children as children of the covenant—yet this does not mean that all our children have already been regenerated by God's Spirit. Listen to his own words:

> You may not let your children grow up without ever letting them think of the obligation of conversion. You may not let them suppose that conversion is something that happens gradually to older people. If you do, you will share in the guilt when your children confess publicly without ever previously thinking of their responsibility for conversion. Every Christian child is to be educated to the conviction that he must repent and turn to God. He should be appropriately educated to this conviction in the manner that is outlined in Question and Answer 88 of the Catechism.[9]

What happened between 1886 and 1892? With all his heart, Kuyper pleaded with his brothers from the Secession not to major in minors but to stress the unity of faith. At a joint meeting held in 1888, he exclaimed:

> Brothers, if the Lord Jesus were in our midst, we would not dare to stay where we are. Let us convene this day as if the

Lord Jesus really were among us. Thank you, brothers, that you have come here from your cities and villages. You did not say: "Leave those 'Doleantie churches' to rule their own affairs." You did not act that way, but you came.[10]

Kuyper wrote and spoke in such a conciliatory manner that, as Dr. Puchinger has recently observed, Kuyper won over many of the men of the Secession by his writings.[11] He certainly remained a beloved servant of God in the opinion of many of them.

The Reformed Churches in The Netherlands became very active in preaching and teaching, in missionary work and in evangelistic and philanthropic activities. As for the old Dutch Reformed Church, she remained what she had long been—a house divided against itself. Yet among her members there were also many who confessed Jesus as Lord and Savior—and some of them voted for Abraham Kuyper when the parliamentary elections rolled around.

Not a Logical Solution

Did Kuyper solve the thorny problem of the purity of the church, or, for that matter, the problem of the unity of the visible church? As we have seen, he was usually very careful in applying the term "false" to a church. He preferred to use expressions like "more or less pure" or even "partly false." And he often spoke of a "pluriformity of churches."

What did he mean by this expression, which was already discussed a great deal during his lifetime and even more after his death? Did he appreciate the multitude of churches the way a child admires the many colors of the rainbow? Was he happy about all the differences in confession and liturgy? Did he like the conflicting statements regarding Christian truth? And did he, in consequence, have to recognize a *pluriformity of the truth*?

In 1901 this last question was put to him straightforwardly by Bensdorp, a Roman Catholic priest who accused him of a "hopeless individualism." According to Bensdorp's understanding, Kuyper believed that the individual was free to adhere to his own conception of the truth, a standpoint which could only lead to conflicting conceptions. Yet, as Bensdorp viewed the matter, Kuyper would consider such conflicting conceptions as the many forms adopted by the one truth.[12]

Bensdorp's question hit home. It reminded people of similar questions that had once been brought to the attention of Protestants by Jacques Bénigne Bossuet, the great French bishop of Meaux who, in his *History of the Variations of the Protestant Churches* (1688), tried to demonstrate that Protestantism could only lead to endless disagreement.

It is unfortunate that Kuyper never found time to write a monograph on this subject. All the same, it is clear that his conception of pluriformity must not be taken to mean that *conflicting* notions of the truth are possible or acceptable. What he had stressed more than once was the necessary variety in types of churches. In 1882 he wrote: "Just as our woods are composed of oaks and elms, of limes and beeches, and cannot be modeled into a shapely clump of nameless trees, so also the cedars of the spiritual Sharon, cannot be changed into uniform plants."[13]

If there is variety in the character of nations (ethnological differences) and in the personal outlook of individuals (psychological differences), it is unavoidable that the life of the church will also be marked by variety. Kuyper speaks somewhere of "the special religious predisposition" of the great races of humanity. The Semites are marked by the fact that they see their God(s) at a great distance; the Japhethites, on the other hand, are inclined toward pantheism. Speaking in very general terms, it can also be said that the Romans, Slavs and Germans felt most at home in their respective Roman Catholic, Greek Catholic and Protestant churches.[14]

There is variety, therefore, and a pluriformity of churches, but this is not the last word: "Satan has succeeded so terribly in breaking up the church of Christ in the world."[15] Here is the other side of the story. It is not the case that every new church is like a fresh ray of sunshine beaming into the world. A new church might also be founded by a "Jeroboam who made Israel to sin."

Kuyper was as much opposed to the forced unity of Rome as to the unrestricted freedom to be found among many Protestant churches. What he wanted was a confessional church, a church that confessed only the name of Christ, the Son of the living God. He wanted the Christ of the Scriptures and the Scriptures of Christ, and that was why he became a reformer of the Dutch Reformed Church in the second half of the nineteenth century. He did not rejoice because the Dutch Reformed Church was trying to express the truth in so many different ways; neither did he say, after the *Doleantie,* that his "lamenting" church and the established church were simply birds of the same feather. He was in total agreement with his friend Prof. F.L. Rutgers, who explained Article 85 of the Dort church order as follows:

> An instituted church without a confession, or a church that abandons the confession, is a human association, one of the many societies of men in which the will of man—rather than the will of the Lord—lays down the law. We cannot recognize such churches; even correspondence with them only weakens the position of our own churches.[16]

Kuyper recognized that the Reformed churches were not the only churches in the world. At the same time, he insisted that any church should be marked by a clear confession of the truth and an unrelenting upholding of that confession. On the other hand, he did sometimes idealize his conception of pluriformity. But it should be added that in all his practical activities he emphasized the necessity of an ongoing reformation of all churches in accordance with the principles of the Word of God.[17]

Chapter 10

The Salt of the Earth: Kuyper and the Social Problem

The Need of the Hour

It is almost a shock. We have witnessed Kuyper's Herculean labors as church leader, politician, editor, and professor. He has expressed a deep wish to do nothing but study theology and publish the results of his study. But in 1891 we find him standing on the platform of an Amsterdam meeting hall, delivering the opening speech at the First Christian Social Congress (in The Netherlands), an organization that came into existence mainly through his efforts.

When we read this speech today, we can see just how well he had studied. He had read not just theology but also sociology. He had consulted the works of the best Roman Catholic authors who dealt with social problems. He had also read the English leaders in this area, and even Marx and Engels. The man who seemed to have no time to spare had made time for social issues.

Kuyper believed that it was the need of the hour. We have seen that he pleaded the cause of the "underdog" in his very first speeches in Parliament. He had spoken up for working men, for women and children. He had also argued the case of parents who wanted to have their children instructed as God's covenant children but could not quite pay for private education.

There had not been much improvement in the situation. The liberal minister Van Houten had enacted a law in 1874 which limited child labor, but a public investigation in 1886 demonstrated that this law had often been evaded. The problem seemed to be a lack of controls. Kuyper had reacted to the investigation by publishing a brochure in 1889 that dealt with manual labor (*Handenarbeid*). In this brochure he emphasized that although control was necessary, it was not enough. Labor itself should be organized in some way and should be able to speak up for itself.

Socialism had meanwhile begun to enter the Low Countries. Domela Nieuwenhuis, a Dutch socialist-anarchist leader, had attended the International Socialist Congress held in Brussels in 1891, which was the same year that Kuyper held his meeting in Amsterdam. Nieuwenhuis proposed that young men everywhere in western Europe be advised to refuse to serve in the army.

Kuyper was well aware of these things in the air. He was convinced that a solution to labor problems could be found only in obedience to Christ. Therefore he organized the congress in Amsterdam.

The Situation

In Kuyper's view, the painful social realities of his time were the result of the ideas of the French Revolution. In his opening address at the congress, entitled "Het sociale vraagstuk en de christelijke religie" ("The Social Question and the Christian Religion"), he tried to demonstrate how those ideas had become prevalent.

The French Revolution was a reaction to the corrupt absolutism of the worldly princes and the corrupt power of the church. The revolution had tried to liberate the third estate. But the liberation turned out to be totally Humanistic and individualistic. The authority of human reason replaced the authority of God and His Word. The reality of organic life created by God and of social ties founded in His covenant was replaced by the autonomy and egoism of the individual.

The result was threefold—a profound social need, a widespread social democratic movement, and a very thorny social problem. The need arose because when the people lacked spiritual nourishment, they became eager for material things. The struggle for life became a struggle for money. The wealthy middle class showed the hardness of the human heart in its attitude toward the proletariat, under the cover of the slogan:

freedom for everyone.

In response, the social democrats pointed out that the *equality* promised by the French revolution had never been realized. They predicted that the oppressed would extort by force what was being taken from them. They would be led to the promised land through revolution.

In essential matters, the social democrats were not much different from the liberals. Like the liberals, they replaced the sovereignty of God with the sovereignty of the people. Moreover, they also denied the essential unity of life. They were well aware of the inequality of the situation of their time; being radicals, they preached the gospel of the class struggle. They were right to identify the social problem, but they were wrong in the solution they offered.

Most Christians of the time were afraid to say anything. They were convinced that we must be satisfied with the situation in which, under God's providence, we live. Also, they did not want to provoke a revolt by the "lower classes." The government should stay out of labor problems, they maintained. Two months before the social congress started, one such conservative Christian had written to Kuyper:

> I am not a proponent of governmental labor regulations. Relations among men should be regulated by state law as little as possible. Religion, sense of duty and humanity are the three factors that should rule the relationship between employers and workmen. The law always limits freedom, which is a particularly dangerous situation in the area of industry and commerce because the limitation is often dangerous to the laborer himself.[1]

This was, and still is, the way many broad-minded Christians think who stand up for the defense of individual rights and for private enterprise and are mortally afraid of any government interference. Kuyper did not agree with him, but neither did he cherish the ideal of an almighty state which would solve the social problem by means of laws and regulations. What did he want, then?

The First Christian Social Congress

The First Christian Social Congress, which met in Amsterdam on November 9-12, 1891, was important for more than one reason. It was important because so many people, both employers and employees, attended. (The number of participants was well over 500.) It was important because a number of questions were discussed in the various workshops. The religious, social and political sides of each question were dealt with. It was also important because the people who attended drew some conclusions that were very radical for the time, such as "the right to strike should not be denied," under the condition that "it never should be used as a political instrument, or as a wanton breach of contract."[2]

The highlight of the congress was Kuyper's address. With great rhetorical power he placed the social problem on the agenda of organized Christianity. Christians, precisely because they are Christians, should feel responsible for the social situation and should do all they can to work toward a solution. "With God's Word in our hands we should vigorously criticize our unhealthy society. We should not rest until that society, apart from government aid, has been reformed in accordance with the Word of God."[3]

What was Kuyper's solution? He pointed to seven fundamental rules.

(1) The first article of our catholic Christian faith must be borne in mind: I believe in God the Father almighty, Maker of heaven and earth. According to Kuyper, this article dominates the entire social problem.[4] God created the whole world and has also provided ordinances for the domain of labor. "We are entirely dependent on those ordinances of God in nature and in the moral law, as His revelation makes them known."

(2) We should make a clear distinction between the authority of the state and the freedom of society. The state is not above everything else, but neither should society be idolized; each has a sovereignty within its own sphere.

(3) We should recognize that human society is not an aggregation of individuals but an organic body. God made us from one blood and made a covenant with man. Man fell—not just individually, but with all his descendants. God then made a new

covenant. All these factors point to the coherent unity of society.

(4) God made us responsible persons who do not leave things as they are in this world simply because God's hand is at work in history. If there are unbearable situations, Christians should do their utmost to change them.

(5) Christians should not join in any revolutionary action that promises a utopia. Instead they should try to build up or renew society gradually.

(6) We should realize that God is the absolute owner of all things and that even the richest man is no more than a steward. God's Word does not call for a community of goods (communism) or declare that the ownership of goods is sacred; what it requires of us is the responsible use of goods. In the organic coherence of humanity there is an organic coherence of goods.

(7) Landed property should not all be in the hands of a minority, for we should remember that God gave the fields of Israel to all the tribes and families of His people. In passing Kuyper mentioned the alarming situation in Scotland, where three-quarters of the landed property was in the hands of fourteen persons. One of the fourteen had recently purchased a new piece of land inhabited by almost 300 people. He ousted the inhabitants because he wanted to turn the land into a new hunting ground. Kuyper exclaimed: "Your own hearts tell you that such a disposal of the land *does* clash with the ordinances of God."

In his speech Kuyper also mentioned God's ordinances for family life, for marriage, and for birth. He declared that according to Scripture, "the laborer deserves his wages" and should enjoy periods of rest. Moreover, he still deserves wages when, in his old age, he is no longer able to work.

Finally, Kuyper stressed that the government should no more take upon itself the tasks of society than society should assume the government's responsibilities. The essential task of the government is the administration of justice. Yet the government should act when one sphere of life infringes on the rights of another sphere. Only in that case shall government interfere; in general, Kuyper was not calling for government interference in labor questions. It would be best, he believed, if labor would organize itself to include both employers and employees. The government could then recognize and protect organized labor by enacting a labor code.

The Test

In 1901, some twenty-five years after the death of the "general without an army" (Groen van Prinsterer), Kuyper became prime minister of The Netherlands. The Free University granted him a leave of absence from his professorial duties, but he continued to write weekly meditations for *The Herald*. He was sixty-four years old—in the prime of his life.

Kuyper was now being put to the test: could and would his political and social ideals be realized, or would it become clear that they were nothing more than castles in the air? In other words, would Abraham Kuyper, the former minister of the Word, really be able to serve as a minister of the crown?

It has often been said that Kuyper's performance in the office of prime minister was a disappointment. Indeed, in terms of social legislation, the harvest was rather scanty, but, as we shall see, there were reasons for this deficiency. Although Kuyper did not achieve all that he set out to do, he was still a powerful and able Christian statesman.

One political-social affair took center stage while Kuyper was prime minister—the general strike of 1903, against which Kuyper introduced legislation. To grasp the importance of this affair, we must first take a look at its background.

It was a time of rising social democracy. Radical, even anarchistic elements played a role in the rise of the new movement. In 1893 the early socialists founded the National Labor Secretariat. In order to generate a climate of class struggle, the Secretariat promoted strikes. Since the waterfront appeared to be the strategic place for strikes it founded a federation of organizations of stevedores in 1900. Whenever one of those organizations went on strike, the others would follow suit. The ultimate goal was a general strike—as a prelude to the establishment of a socialist state.

The signal was given in 1903. There was a strike at an Amsterdam dock company; immediately railroad workers became involved. The socialist leader Peter Jelles Troelstra coined the slogan: "All the machinery stands still / At the impulse of your will." On February 3, 1903, a manifesto appeared. It contained the message that all the railroad workers would go on strike as soon as the signal was given. This could lead to a general strike and usher in "the dictatorship of the proletariat."[5]

It was an alarming situation. What would the government do? On February 24, Prime Minister Kuyper proposed three bills in the Dutch House of Commons. The first one prohibited strikes by public servants. The second required that a railroad brigade be available to ensure that essential services would not be interrupted. And the third called for the establishment of an investigative committee to look into the legal status and job security of the railroad workers.

Kuyper had already defended these drastic measures in *De Standaard,* his newspaper. He had written about the original strike in Amsterdam and had admitted that it was legitimate, given the circumstances. But he added that when the railroad workers came into the picture, the original strike became a political weapon in the hands of the socialists. To Kuyper this was the beginning of a *coup d'état.* Unless curbed, such measures could be taken virtually at any time by the socialists. This Kuyper regarded as intolerable.[6] When he defended his proposals in Parliament, he expressed the same ideas:

> No one in this government wants reactionary measures. Neither the government nor the House of Commons will stop urging reformation of our social conditions. But the ship of state will not be taken over with our acquiescence. In the well-understood interest of all parties, the authority of the law will be powerfully maintained.[7]

Kuyper's point was clear: there had to be reformation of the often reprehensible labor conditions, but there was to be no class struggle, no abuse of the sharp weapon of strikes.

Kuyper's bills passed with an overwhelming majority. Yet this situation hampered the legislative work of his cabinet. There were also other critical matters claiming much of his attention, such as the illness of the queen and the question of succession which it raised, the Boer War, and the war between Russia and Japan.

Even so, Kuyper achieved some remarkable things. He certainly proved that he was the man who "possessed ten heads and a hundred arms." (This was how he was described in the *Algemeen Handelsblad,* the leading liberal paper, on April 22, 1897.) Among his accomplishments were the elementary education bill (the Christian schools received more government subsidy), the bill for technological higher education (the famous school in Delft was granted university status), and the bill that granted the Free University of Amsterdam public status equal to that of the other universities.

A small but very important feature of his term of office was the compassion he showed to widows and orphans. One day a committee representing teaching organizations had an audience with Prime Minister Kuyper in order to ask for pensions. Kuyper said to them: "Why don't you ask the same for your widows?" They asked and received—and their orphans were included as well. The same spirit was present in Kuyper's proposed workman's insurance bill which covered sickness, disability, and old age: the bill also covered widows. Kuyper prepared legislation that expanded the protection of women and young people in industry, and he broadened the coverage of the Workman's Compensation Law.

Kuyper certainly tried to practice what he had long preached, but his days as prime minister were numbered. The socialists hated him, and the liberals considered him their sworn enemy. Thus, before he was able to carry his program through to completion, he was defeated in the election of 1905. He retired from office, and a liberal cabinet was sworn in.

According to P. Kasteel, his Roman Catholic biographer, the real reason for Kuyper's defeat was the fact that he had made the *antithesis* (i.e. the contrast between the Christian worldview and the Humanistic worldview) the basis of his politics.[8] It was said that he tried to divide the country into two hostile camps. Kuyper replied that he had not created the antithesis; he had simply found it. There *are* persons who respect Christ as King in the totality of life, and there *are* others who don't, who may perhaps reserve a corner of their heart for Him and thus have some feeling for Him but do not confess that unto Him all authority has been given. It is still true that "he who is not with Him is against Him" (Matt. 12:30).

His Last Blast

Kuyper died in 1920, some fifteen years after leaving the office of prime minister. Two years before his death, when he was eighty-one years old, he attended a meeting of delegates of the local electoral associations.* The delegates at this meeting were Christians who were aware of their political responsibility and formed the backbone of his party.

Kuyper customarily set the tone at these meetings by exhorting the party members in his famous "deputy speeches." He had prepared a speech for the meeting of 1918, but he was eighty-one years old and his voice had become too weak for him to deliver it. Therefore his speech was read by Idenburg, the former governor-general of Indonesia, who was a good friend of his.

This speech was Kuyper's last blast. It was vintage Kuyper but also the speech of an old man, lacking some power and focus. Still, one thing stood out—his emphasis on the importance of solving the *social* problem.

The title of the speech was "What Now?" There were at least three reasons to ask this question. The first one was that the end of the first world war seemed near. A host of problems were becoming visible in the wake of that war—especially economic problems.

The second reason was that Bolshevism had begun to conquer Russia. Kuyper declared that Soviet communism was worse than the Jacobinism of the French Revolution. The slogan of 1789 had been "No God and no master." In 1917 the Soviets added: "No God-given structures of life, no law and order." And they would be able to maintain their hold on the nation only through tyrannical elitism.** This was a sign of the times.

The third reason was that the school problem had been solved. One of the major struggles of Kuyper's life had ended in complete victory. Free Christian schools were not only funded by the government, but were considered completely equal to the public schools. This was a great victory indeed, but the aged Kuyper now asked: What now? Did the party exist only to win legal equality for the Christian schools? Can we leave the burning questions in the world to be solved by the world's experts? Do we still have a task?

---

* Dutch: *kiesvereniging*. The annual meeting of delegates was called the *deputatenvergadering*.

** In Kuyper's words: "A group of dictatorial individuals force their will upon the whole country" (*Wat nu?*, p. 9).

Kuyper answered his own question by emphasizing as strongly as he could that Christians must still work toward the solution of the social problem. He pointed out that the laborer had gained much status in the fifty years past. He had become more educated. The work of Christian labor unions had demonstrated that there were men of clear insight and great capacity to be found among Christian workers.

Those Christian unions should not serve the interests of their own class only. They should not only be socially oriented but should cooperate with all their fellow Christians in building up the totality of life. "The water of life from the one fountain should irrigate family life, social life and political life."[9] And all of this was to be done to the honor of God. "This has been the starting point of our power, and this should remain, to the end, the sanctified inspiration of all our efforts."

Chapter 11

Professor Kuyper

"My dear boy"

This was Kuyper's usual form of address to one of his students. Rev. Taeke Ferwerda, who studied under Kuyper and was put to death by the Germans on September 12, 1944, has recorded this detail for posterity. The students respected and revered him. In fact, they loved him with a very special love.

He taught them the rudiments of the Hebrew language. He also taught them the principles of aesthetics. He himself was an artist with words. He was careful to point out the relationship between Calvinism and art. (On this subject, see the fifth chapter of his book *Calvinism*.) When he taught dogmatics, he began by pointing to the eternal counsel of God and to the glory of God. He tried to show the connections between all the parts of salvation.

Kuyper also taught a homiletics class, a class to teach students how to preach. It was in connection with this class that they had personal contact with him. The students, by turns, would receive a text from Kuyper. A week later the student would have to appear at Kuyper's house with the outline of a sermon based on that text.

When the student appeared at his home, Kuyper would take his time: for ten minutes he would read the outline with concentrated attention. Then he would talk to the student, often taking the tone of a father chastening his child. Let us listen to the words directed to his student Ferwerda on such an occasion:

> My dear boy, you have constructed a pretty good outline. It is a well-ordered whole, logically it runs smoothly, there isn't a

single weak spot in it,—but you can't preach this way! Do you
know what I myself usually do when I am preparing to write a
sermon or a meditation? I start by forming an idea of what
Scripture tells us in the text I have in mind. When I see the idea
sharply, I listen to the voices in my own heart that protest
against it. Then I wrestle with those voices until I have silenced
them, before the Word of God. Such a sermon is not always
completely logical, and there may seem to be inconsistencies
here and there, but, my dear boy, only then do you start
preaching.[1]

Professor Kuyper was a staunch defender of the church's
confessions, and the situation of his church warranted his strong
confessional stand. Kuyper tried to display the beauty of the
church's dogmas as reflections of the thoughts of God. Yet he
was no dogmatist, nor was he an intellectualist. In the voice of
the preacher he wanted to hear what came from the heart. What
should come through in a sermon was that the preacher had
wrestled with God. This was one of the reasons why his students
loved him. We listen again to Ferwerda:

When Kuyper lectured, his students felt prompted not just to
listen to him but also to see him. He seemed to be a living
source of energy. When he made a dogma known to his
students, it was not a dry abstraction or a piece of intellectual
speculation or scholastic hair-splitting; no, it *lived*. The
problems that arose in our minds were not evaded but were
met foursquare. It was an exciting procedure, and the end
result was not, as some naive minds might have surmised, that
the problems were solved: they were laid in the hands of God.
The mighty thinker always remained a child bowing in humility before the Word of God.

A good example of Kuyper's style is his treatment of the
doctrine of predestination. Kuyper was a supralapsarian and, as
we have noted, has been reproached for this.[2] Supralapsarianism, together with its counterpart infralapsarianism, were
discussed a great deal by Reformed theologians in the period
before the Synod of Dort (1618-19). What was the difference
between these two positions? They both recognized the fact that
Scripture teaches God's unconditional predestination, but they
differed on the *object* of that predestination. Was the object
man, or *fallen* man? In other words, did God elect His own
before the fall (supra), "from the foundation of the world," or
did He do so *after* the fall (infra)? The Synod of Dort chose the

infralapsarian position,[3] but it did not condemn supralapsarianism. (Anyone who supposes that the differences between the two positions is merely a matter of hair-splitting should be reminded of the fact that what is at stake is not just an issue in systematic theology but also the plain exegesis of certain texts, such as Revelation 13:8 and Ephesians 1:4.)

When we judge Kuyper's thinking by his overall theological stance we have to call him a supralapsarian. He always stressed the absolute sovereignty of God. Yet, in contrast to his teacher Scholten, he was not a determinist. He made a point of emphasizing the inadequacy of our knowledge of these matters. Hence he argued that neither supralapsarianism nor infralapsarianism is able to solve the riddle that on the one hand man is genuinely and totally responsible for the fall into sin, while on the other hand the fall represented the fulfillment of God's eternal counsel. He wrote:

> The point is that we should distinguish between that which we can explain because it is revealed to us and that which we cannot explain because it is higher than our understanding. And then all believers should stand firm in their conviction that the connection between God's eternal good counsel and the fall of man is inscrutable for us. If we were to move logically from God's decree to the fall, there would be no *guilt* any more. But if we were to move logically from the fall to the decree, we would lose our God. All the systems that tried to solve this problem ended by either weakening our feeling of guilt or weakening our confession of the freedom and perfection of God.[4]

Students were often moved as they listened to Kuyper lecture. One of Kuyper's students was A.G. Honig, who later became a professor at Kampen. In his doctoral dissertation Honig compared Kuyper's lectures to the inspiring words of Luther and to the powerful products of Calvin's mind. Honig felt moved to express his gratitude to God ". . . because He in His grace gave a noble man like you to Calvinist Holland, a man who honors all that is truly human and is a reformer in the areas of aesthetics, literature, science, church, and society."[5] Another of the appreciative students was Abraham Kuyper, Jr., who wrote in the introduction to his dissertation:

> Through your catechetical instruction, Calvinism has had the love of my heart for a long time already, and through your

academic instruction that love climbed to its zenith. God has given you the grace and the lasting honor of being the regenerator of Calvinism in our century. 'Soli Deo Gloria' has always been your motto. The glory of God in all areas of life—that was what you always impressed upon the minds of your disciples.[6]

The Making of a Student

On two occasions Kuyper delivered a special address to his students on the character and method of their studies. The first time was in 1889, when he opened the lessons with a speech on "Scholastica, or the secret of real study." In this speech he declared that real study is marked by the fact that it is related to God and to man. It is related to God in that the true student is like a miner who digs up the gold of God's creation. And it is related to man because the products of his study should serve mankind.

There is only one way to be, or to become, a real student. In a "Method of Study"[7] designed especially for theological students, Kuyper provided a blueprint for what he had in mind. He spoke of three conditions.

First, the *spiritual* condition is regeneration or being born again. Regeneration becomes evident in the daily conversion of one's heart and life to God.

Secondly, the *ethical* condition is the requirement of obedience, patience and self-control—in short, unconditional obedience to Christ. Kuyper called for persistent patience in the face of any and all difficulties, and for a prayerful self-control that says, "Not my will but Thine be done."

Thirdly, there were *intellectual* requirements to be met. First of all, one had to be the graduate of a Latin school (Dutch: *gymnasium*) and have completed two years of preparatory studies in such fields as ancient languages, history and philosophy. Kuyper then outlined an extensive program adding up to four years of the study of theology.

Kuyper opened the academic lessons of 1900 with another address called "Scholastica." This time the subtitle was "For the sake of seeking or finding?" Apparently Kuyper was well aware of the great influence on modern theology the German philosopher, Lessing (1729-1781) had. Lessing had made the famous statement: "Not the finding, but the seeking, of truth is the goal of true Science."

In his speech Kuyper granted that there is great pleasure in seeking: he pointed to sportsmen, hunters and fishermen who delight in the pursuit of their quarry. But seeking, he declared, remains an empty or vain business if there is no fulfillment in finding. The thirsty man is not content with finding the source only, he must *drink* the water to quench his thirst.

Kuyper ended the speech by laying down some principles. The first was that we should not seek what we already have. In other words, we should not follow Descartes' advice and doubt everything that our eyes see and our senses experience.*

The second principle was that we should not seek what others have already found. This means that we should start with history, appreciating the work of God-given forerunners and taking our place in the succession of the times. The third presupposition was that we should not seek what God has given us already, that is, the truth revealed to us in His holy Word. Scripture should be the basis of all scientific instruction.

Philosophy

Strictly speaking, Kuyper was not a philosopher. That is to say, he was not a man who pondered life's deepest problems, nor was he a sage who speculated about the hidden depths of the universe or the human heart. He was rather a man of action in church and state and society—in all areas of life, as he used to say.

Academically speaking, he was a theologian, a master in historical theology and a grand master in dogmatics. Yet his was a universal spirit: he was never caught up in any specialty. He loved to present the whole world to his students as the "glorious theater of the works of God."

---

* In his *Lectures on Calvinism* delivered in 1898, Kuyper declared: "The presupposition of all scientific knowledge is belief in our own being, in our own senses; belief in the correctness of the law of thinking; belief in the general aspect of the special phenomena; above all, belief in the principles that lead us" (*Het Calvinisme*, 1899, p. 124).

In this regard he was a true Calvinist. Calvin was the one who had said: "It is fitting for man seriously to turn his eyes to contemplate God's works, since he has been placed in this most glorious theater to be a spectator of them," and also that man should therefore "prick up his ears to the Word, the better to profit."[8]

One of the academic subjects dearest to Kuyper's heart was his "encyclopedia of sacred theology." He was concerned even more broadly with an "encyclopedia of science," by which he understood a theory of learning in which the organic structure of reality is expounded, together with the corresponding organic structure of scientific thinking. The results of his lectures on these topics are recorded in his three-volume *Encyclopedia of Sacred Theology*, an enormous work.

The first part is a detailed historical review of all the efforts made over the ages to organize knowledge, especially theological knowledge. In the second part Kuyper presents his own theory of knowledge. In the third part he gives a systematic description of the organism of theology.

Why is scientific knowledge so important? The highest goal of the scientific enterprise is to find out and rethink the thoughts of God as expressed in the creation. How is such a thing possible? Man has been created by God in His image as a kind of microcosm of the cosmos. In all of his being he is related to the cosmos as a whole, and this is why he is able to form a mental conception of the cosmos in its organic coherence.

The study of nature is not a luxury. We are all called to honor God, and it is the special vocation of people possessing scientific ability to explore the structure of creation. In the process they discover God's greatness, which they then express in human thought and words.[9]

God originally created the universe as a *cosmos*, a well-structured whole. In spite of the destruction wrought by sin, we can still speak of laws of nature. (Kuyper stresses that these laws are not given *by* nature but *to* nature.) God preserves His own works in His common grace, and in His special grace He saves them.

In science there are different schools of thought, just as there are different communities of insight into God's revelation. (Kuyper points repeatedly to the different patterns of thinking in the Roman Catholic, Greek Catholic, Lutheran, and Calvinist communities.) On one side of the line of division we find the *normalists,* and on the other side the *abnormalists.* The normalists maintain that the cosmos we live in, that is, mankind together with the entire world, is following a normal and natural course. Kuyper observes:

> They refuse to go beyond the natural givens. They never give up until they have found the same fundamental explanation for all phenomena; they always look only for the logical consequences of cause and effect. *Formally* speaking, therefore, they have some sort of faith, but only in the contents of their own consciousness viewed as normal. *Materially* speaking, they believe not in creation but in evolution, without beginning and without end. Not a single species—not even homo sapiens—has an origin of its own; each one has developed within the circle of the natural givens, from lower and preceding species. Miracles are impossible; natural law reigns relentlessly. There is no sin, but there is development from a lower and preceding species. Scripture may be respected, but only after we have first cut out anything that cannot be logically explained from a human point of view. Christ may be honored, but only as a product of all that is human in Israel. It is possible that there is a God—or rather, an infinite being—but only hidden between all the visible things in an agnostic manner, or present in all existing things in an agnostic manner, or present in all existing things in a pantheistic manner, and as nothing more than an ideal reflections of the human spirit.

This is Kuyper's thumbnail sketch of the normalists, who are the leading scientists of his time. What about the abnormalists? He writes:

> The *abnormalists* do not deny that there is such a thing as limited (micro)evolution, but because of their faith in creation they reject an evolution in infinitum. They stick inexorably to the notion of man as an irreducible species, for the image of God is reflected in him. Sin has disturbed the sinless origin of man and was a transgression against God. Therefore only re-creation can restore that which became abnormal, which means that miracles were necessary—the miracle of regeneration, the miracle of Scripture, the miracle of the Christ, when God Himself descended with His own life into our life.[10]

Earlier we noted that Kuyper posited regeneration as a necessary condition for a man to become a real scientist. We also observed that he believed the antithesis to be operative everywhere in public life. We now see that he made it clear to his students that these terms were not his own special jargon but stood for unavoidable realities.

Theology

Did Kuyper develop a special theology of his own? This question cannot be answered with a simple yes or a simple no.

Kuyper certainly did not aim to develop a new or unique theology. More than once he declared that he was no more than a copyist: "I am not original; I am only copying. What I am aiming at in my theological and political activities is simply to present a copy of what Calvin and his school were aiming at."[11]

All he really wanted was to be a Reformed historical theologian. As he had put it some years earlier:

> We don't make any progress when we keep founding new trends and schools. All those parties and factions are detrimental to our spiritual life. Our persons ought to go more to the background—then the church of Christ will become more visible. We are following the safest route when we proceed from the doctrine of our fathers as it was confessed until about 1750; in a healthy way and adorned with solid knowledge, we should follow this route in our schools and houses of prayer, in our homes and our personal meditations.[12]

In an American journal of those years, Herman Bavinck wrote in the same vein about Kuyper's theology:

> Avoiding all Apologetics, Dr. Kuyper proceeded in a thetical manner. He chose his standpoint not on the outside but within faith, planted himself squarely on the basis of the infallible Scriptures and the Reformed Confession. His arms were directed not against the unbelieving enemies without, but against the heterodox friends within. Incessantly in his weekly paper, *De Heraut,* the reigning orthodoxy was exposed, as to the weakness of its principle, its departure from the Reformed Confession, its destructive tendencies. The result was that the followers of Van Oosterzee, Doedes, and de la Saussaye became more and more estranged from Kuyper.
>
> While thus embracing the Reformed doctrine he revives the same in its most strict type. To him the line marked by the names of Calvin, Voetius, Comrie represents Reformed

theology in its most correct development. For it is characteristic of the Reformed doctrine, that it deduces all things from God and makes all things return to God. Hence Dr. Kuyper is not satisfied until every dogma has been traced to its deepest roots and set forth in its inner connection with the divine decree. He never remains on the surface, but goes down into the deep region of principles, seeking to penetrate through the phenomena into the sphere of the noumena. It would be unjust, therefore, to say that Dr. Kuyper's work confines itself to a mere repristination and slavish reproduction of the old Reformed models. He does not produce a new theology, but reproduces the old in an independent and sometimes a free manner. The various Reformed doctrines are to him not loosely connected *loci communes,* but, being most intimately related, they form one world of ideas, one strictly coherent system. This system, with its firmly drawn, clear lines of thought, reproduced from the writings of the best Reformed theologians, he endeavors to accredit and recommend to the children of our age, tossed to and fro by every wind of doctrine.[13]

Bavinck did not always agree with Kuyper,[14] but he never doubted the genuinely Reformed character of his theology.

On the other hand, there is something uniquely Kuyperian to be found on every page of Kuyper's theological writings. Kuyper had a unique personal style which often had a rhetorical ring. His powerful imagination enabled him to see things in a new way and to render abstract ideas concrete. And his *architectonic* talents drove him always to arrange things in well-ordered wholes.

To Kuyper, the heart of theology is the knowledge of God as He has revealed Himself in His holy Word. That Word, the sacred Scripture inspired by the Holy Spirit and understood through the illumination of that same Spirit, is the point of departure in classifying the various theological disciplines.

Kuyper recognized four classes of theological disciplines. First of all, there are the *bibliological* disciplines, which aim at deepening and increasing our knowledge of the Bible itself. They are in turn divided into canonical disciplines (the Bible as a book), exegetical disciplines (the Bible as writing), and

---

* Kuyper did, however, recognize the right and necessity of sound Reformed apologetics (see *Encyclopaedia*, III, pp. 456 ff).

pragmatic disciplines (the Bible as witness). Pragmatical subjects are sacred archeology, biblical history, and the history of revelation.

The second class of theological disciplines are the *ecclesiological* ones, which demonstrate the effect of the witness of the Bible on the origin and existence of the church. They are divided into institutional and organic disciplines. Institutional subjects are juridical (canon law or church order), historical (church history), and statistical (church statistics). The organic subjects focus on the knowledge of Christian personal life, organized life (family, society and state), and non-organized life (in science, literature and art).

The third group are the *dogmatological* disciplines, which show how Scripture has been reflected in the dogma of the church. They are to be divided into diathetical subjects,* (study of the confessions and of the history of dogma), thetical subjects (dogmatics and ethics), and antithetical subjects (polemics, elenchtics and apologetics).

The fourth group are the *diaconological* subjects, which show us how the Word of God is to be administered by the office-bearers. (The Greek word *diakonia* means office.) This group is to be divided into didaskalian subjects (a "didaskalos" is a teacher), presbyterial subjects, and diaconal subjects; we should also add the subjects that are related to the office of all believers (laical subjects).

Kuyper was not only the architect who had designed this blueprint for the edifice of theology; he joined his students in entering the rooms one by one to show them how they should live in each room to the glory of God. In other words, he kept making clear the task of the real theologian in all the details of his field of study.

Neo-Calvinism?

From different sides and for quite different reasons, Kuyper has been accused of being a *neo* Calvinist. This term means not just a renewal of original Calvinism but also a devia-

---

* By "diathetical" Kuyper means the situation and nature of a thing.

tion from it. To put it in crude terms, the term means that Kuyper pretended to be a Calvinist when he really wasn't.[15]

Ernst Troeltsch, the well-known author of *The Social Teachings of the Christian Churches,* discussed neo-Calvinism extensively and drew the following conclusion:

> Neo-Calvinism, with its Free Church system, and its accompanying phenomena of democracy and liberalism, as well as with the pietistic rigorism of a strong, self-controlled individualism, very utilitarian in secular affairs, has moved far away from the early aristocratic Calvinism of the period of its formation in Geneva, when it was still close to Lutheranism.[16]

Two points stand out here: first, that Calvin would not have been a free church man, as Kuyper was, and secondly that Kuyper was characterized by pietistic rigorism.

Is there any truth to this accusation? Could it be that Kuyper was not the Calvinist he pretended to be?

The absurdity of such an indictment is clear as soon as we compare Kuyper to J.H. Scholten, his teacher. Scholten certainly claimed to be a Calvinist; in his major work he left the impression (and there is no reason to doubt his sincerity) that he was upholding the doctrine of the Dutch Reformed church in his reinterpretation of it. But because of his philosophical views, the doctrine of predestination was transformed into a cold determinism, while the doctrine of the testimony of the Holy Spirit was changed into that of our own human mind and conscience.

By contrast, in all his teaching, Kuyper was *issu de Calvin.* * After having tried out the various modern and mediating theologies of his time, he finally found rest for his heart in the God-honoring, Christ-centered Scriptural theology of the great Geneva reformer.

We should not forget that Troeltsch, despite his brilliant insights, was a liberal philosopher who had his own special image of Calvin. Moreover, Troeltsch had only read one or two of Kuyper's books. It should not surprise us that he drew a sharp contrast between the stern reformer of Geneva, whose elders were chosen from the city council and who was averse to any form of toleration, and Kuyper, the leader of a Dutch secession

---

* Literally: issued from Calvin. This expression was often used by Groen van Prinsterer.

church and opponent of the idea of a national church. Troeltsch did not take proper account of the difference between deviation and development.

Is it really true that Calvin was in favor of one national church? And was Kuyper a man of pietistic secession? In Geneva, Calvin had fought one of the great battles of his life to make the church free from the state. Moreover, he wanted the council of the church to have the right to discipline apart from or even contrary to the will of, the city council. And when Calvinism began to spread everywhere, minority churches were established—in France, Belgium, Germany, and England. Calvin was more tolerant of the Lutheran churches than they were of him. He even found traces of the true church among the Roman Catholics.[17]

And what about Kuyper's so-called pietistic rigorism? It seems strange to hear Kuyper contrasted with Calvin on this point, especially because Calvin has so often been accused of a rigorous ethical asceticism. Kuyper shared that attitude to a certain extent: he stood in the Calvinist tradition of opposition to dancing, card-playing and theater-going.[18] On the other hand, by virtue of his doctrine of "common grace" he stressed the enjoyment of God's gifts in all areas of life more than Calvin had done.[19]

The heart of Troeltsch's criticism is that Kuyper, the man of the "Doleantie," was a pietist who chose for a small church instead of an encompassing state church. In his emphasis on regeneration, moreover, there is an individualistic attitude.

It would be very easy to demonstrate that Kuyper, especially in his doctrine of the church, was not a pietist at all. He was not comforted by the solace of pious prayer meetings; instead he wanted the entire church, with all its members, to be alive and active.

It is true, however, that Kuyper stressed personal regeneration. It is in connection with this subject that a second group of critics accused him of "neo-Calvinism." Members of the original Secession churches in The Netherlands and in the United States objected to Kuyper's "speculations," his "scholastic method," and his alleged use of unwarranted assumptions. Among the Dutch critics were Rev. T. Bos and Prof. L. Lindeboom; chief among the American critics were

Rev. L.J. Hulst and Prof. F.M. ten Hoor.

The objections they raised were not altogether unfounded. Kuyper had an exceedingly logical mind, and once he started reasoning there was no stopping him. At the same time, the objections were not altogether to the point. Kuyper did hold the supralapsarian position, but in the end he confessed that no human mind is able to fathom the secrets of God.

As Kuyper dealt with the subject of justification, dear to the heart of every Reformed Christian, he taught that we are justified by faith only, and through grace. Yet he added (as various Reformed theologians before him had done) that God has decided from all eternity that there should be such justification; he called this divine decree "justification from eternity." Some of his opponents accused him of preferring eternal ideas to historical facts. This was not true, for Kuyper defended the historical facts tooth and nail against all the idealistic theologians of his time, whom he branded pantheists. But he did sometimes skate on thin ice with his logic.

He also took up the difficult subject of "presumptive regeneration," as it has come to be called. As we saw earlier, the fact of our regeneration, our being centrally and totally changed by the Holy Spirit, was a major theme of all his Christian thinking and acting. But what was this presumptive or presumed regeneration?

The problem with the notion of such regeneration had arisen in connection with the baptism of infants. In his days in the Dutch national church, Kuyper had seen how this ceremony had become a dead custom. He opposed the Roman Catholic doctrine of baptismal regeneration just as much the Baptist rejection of infant baptism. The common Reformed position, as expressed in the liturgical form used for infant baptism, was that children should be baptized because they are included in the covenant of grace and share in the promises of that covenant. But Kuyper explained the phrase "sanctified in Christ," which is used in the baptismal form, to mean that children are considered to be born again; in other words, it is presupposed that they are born again. They are so considered because it was not all Israel that was called Israel. Even so, they are born again because baptism is the "washing of regeneration."

Kuyper's position on this matter, which was sometimes unduly and unwisely stressed by some of his disciples, caused a good deal of friction in the Dutch Reformed churches and also in the Christian Reformed Church of North America.[20] Peace finally returned in 1905 when the Synod of Utrecht adopted the following conclusion:

> Synod declares that, according to the Confession of our Churches, the seed of the covenant must, in virtue of the promise of God, be presumed to be regenerated and sanctified in Christ, until as they grow up, the contrary appears from their life or doctrine. That it is, however, less correct to say that baptism is administered to the children of believers on the ground of their presumptive regeneration, since the ground of baptism is the command and the promise of God; and that further the judgment of charity, with which the Church presumes the seed of the covenant to be regenerated, by no means intends to say that therefore each child is really regenerated, since the Word of God teaches that they are not all Israel that are of Israel, and it is said of Isaac: in him shall thy seed be called (Rom. 9:6, 7), so that in preaching it is always necessary to insist on serious self-examination, since only those who shall have believed and have been baptized will be saved.[21]

Symphony

Sometimes Professor Kuyper seemed unpredictable. As we have seen, he seemed to be a severe taskmaster for students who were delivering their first sermon. But once in a while it would happen that "when a student, in the estimate of his fellow students, presented more of a heart-to-heart talk than an opening of the Word, he would be criticized by the professor in a very kindly way—to the amazement of everyone—because he had spoken to the heart of Jerusalem."[22]

Kuyper was a logical thinker, a practical organizer, and a man who stressed personal contact with God. As a result, he has been called a logicist, an activist, and a spiritualist in turn. He did not want to be any one of these. Instead, he strove for a balanced worldview and a balanced presentation of the whole truth of God.

In 1901 he published an excellent book entitled *Three Little Foxes*. He borrowed the title from a text in the Song of Solomon: "Catch us the foxes, the little foxes that spoil the vineyards, for our vineyards are in blossom" (2:15). Were the little foxes spoiling the vineyard of the Reformed churches of his time? He named them: practicism, emotionalism and intellectualism.

> In the first place, the *practicism* that neglects the intellectual element in our religion, does not concern itself with the soundness of the confession, is indifferent to heresies, and does not appreciate mysticism, but abounds in (I will not say good works, for real good works belong in another category) 'Christian activities.' Philanthropy, missions, evangelism, asceticism, all kinds of associations—to begin with, the Sunday school. Always busy, always doing something. Especially eager to do something special.
>
> In the second place, the *emotionalism* that obviously follows two tracks. On the one hand, the deeper emotional way of mysticism; on the other hand, the superficial way of some affection of our feeling. People who take these paths are no more interested in the confession and exploration of the truth than are the followers of practicism. They even welcome preachers who have abandoned Scripture, as long as they lose themselves in the mysticism of the soul, stir the feelings, and move the imagination.
>
> In the third place, the *intellectualism* that has not the slightest understanding of all the fuss about Christian activity. It haughtily despises all emotionalism and does not understand mysticism. On the other hand, it upholds the confession, does not condone any violation of Scripture, and smells any heresy when it begins to appear.

In this beautiful book, Kuyper offers a penetrating analysis of all three attitudes. He concludes with the following summary statement:

> Although I have seriously warned against dry, complacent intellectualism, I do not dispute that it is the duty of Christianity to conceive of and digest the truth of God and to arrive at a clear and lucid conception of what it confesses.
>
> Although I warned against the unbridled error of unhealthy mysticism, I do not deny the calling of the child of God to know what is going on in his soul, to observe what is living in his heart, and to test the experience of the truth in his own spirit.
>
> And also, although I pointed to the serious danger of looking for real Christianity in some extra-Christian activities, no one should conclude that I am advocating quietism—doing nothing and avoiding all good works.
>
> I aimed only at the restoration of a proper harmony. I urged the harmonious development of our Christian existence. I wanted to remove anything that might tip the right balance in

the lives of many. My desire was to arouse love for the higher position, which is a product of an equitable development of our thinking, feeling and active life.

Jesus told us to love God with all our heart, all our mind, all our soul, and all our power. It is often regrettable that our love of God draws on only one or two of these faculties, and that we neglect or don't use the other ones. This causes a defective, imperfect and one-sided development.

What it should be or become is "mature manhood in Christ, when each part is working properly" (Eph. 4).

Chapter 12

In the New World

Recognition

In his excellent biography of Kuyper, Dr. P. Kasteel points out that although Kuyper was held in high esteem among "his own people," he never received from his countrymen in general the recognition to which he was entitled. No Dutch university conferred an honorary degree upon him. Despite his outstanding qualities and service, he was often given the cold shoulder. There was only one exception: the Technical School of Delft, which had been elevated to university status through his efforts, made him *doctor honoris causa* in 1905.

In 1898, however, something very special happened to Kuyper. Two years before, Princeton University in New Jersey had invited him to deliver the Stone Lectures. Now came an additional honor: the University wished to confer an honorary Doctor of Laws degree on him.

Often a prophet is without honor in his own country. Kuyper was deeply moved to be received with open arms in the United States. For some time he had been expressing special fondness for this country.

Attraction of America

It might be said that Kuyper idealized America. He believed that there he could see that dream that he carried in his heart. In his Amsterdam inaugural sermon of 1873, he pointed to the United States as the country of freedom. At the same time he

emphasized that the Americans were a thoroughly religious people, and quoted from Tocqueville's *Democracy in America* in
support of this claim.[1]

In his book on the political program for the Anti-
Revolutionary Party, he expressed a preference for the
Republican Party in America, as opposed to the Democratic
Party. He pictured the Republicans as the spiritual children of
the Pilgrim Fathers, as the heroes of the Civil War, as the op-
ponents of Rome, and as the real American citizens.[2]

In his treatise on the reformation of the churches, Kuyper
pointed out that all the citizens of the American States had the
right to vote, just as the citizens of France did. Still, there was an
important difference. The French considered their suffrage to be
an inborn human right, whereas the citizen of America said: "I
don't vote because of my human right, but by the grace of God,
who has granted me this privilege."[3]

This is not the whole story.[4] But it is certainly clear that
Kuyper looked to America as a country with high civil, political
and spiritual standards and practices. How did he arrive at this
judgment?

We have taken note of a speech he delivered in 1874 in
which he tried to demonstrate that only Calvinism makes real
freedom possible. He said that this historical fact was illustrated
most clearly in the United States. But there are prior sources for
this prospensity in Kuyper's thinking.

From 1869 on, Kuyper was deeply influenced by the works
of Edmund Burke, that great friend of America. It was in 1869
that Kuyper met Groen, and he was eager to take up contact
with more Christian statesmen or to read their works. Hence he
wrote a letter to Groen, who had quoted Burke often in his
Unbelief and Revolution, asking him for the name of a reliable
biography of Burke. Groen sent him several of the latest books
on Burke, and Kuyper profited by reading them. He was very
busy with a thousand and one things, however, and so it was not
until March 7, 1873 that he could write: "I profited from my ailment by reading the entire Burke. I enjoyed it very much."[5]

The entire Burke! Then Kuyper must certainly have read
Burke's famous speech on reconciliation with America. In this
speech Burke pleaded with his countrymen to halt the senseless
war against their own flesh and blood, and he pointed to "the

fierce spirit of liberty which was probably stronger in the English colonies than in any other people of the earth.'' Why this strong spirit of liberty? In the first place, Burke said, the colonists were descendents of Englishmen. However, Burke went on to lay special emphasis on the fact that they were Protestants: ''The people are Protestants, and that of a kind which is the most adverse to all implicit submission of mind and opinion.'' He also wrote: ''All Protestantism is a sort of dissent. But the religion most prevalent in our northern colonies is a refinement on the principle of resistance: it is the dissidence of dissent and the protestantism of the Protestant religion.''[6]

In Kuyper's view, that consistent Protestantism was Calvinism. He had dealt with this theme in his speech of 1874, which appeared in translation in the *Bibliotheca Sacra* in 1895.[7] And it was in this conviction that he landed in America in October of 1898.

Eye to Eye

He was received with open arms. In the month of December, the Presbyterian minister W.H. Roberts, speaking for a committee of ministers drawn from ten different Presbyterian and Reformed denominations, addressed the following words to Kuyper: ''The committee expresses its happiness about the presence of Professor Abraham Kuyper of the Reformed Churches of The Netherlands, whom it honors as one of the greatest thinkers and most influential preachers of the Reformed churches of Europe.''[8] The occasion for these remarks was a lecture Kuyper delivered to the Historical Presbyterian Society.

In June of that same year, the famous Princeton professor Benjamin B. Warfield called Kuyper ''probably the most important person both in state and church in The Netherlands.'' He went on to say:

> For many years he has exercised a most remarkable influence in his own country. Leader and organizer of the Antirevolutionary Party; editor-in-chief of *De Standaard*; founder, defender and soul of the Free University of Amsterdam; consistent advocate of spiritual freedom in the church, and of the

rights of the confession and the principles of the Reformed truth, to which the Dutch people owe all that has promoted their greatness; teacher of religion who feeds thousands of hungry people with his instruction in *De Heraut,* his weekly, and whose lectures at the Free University have shaped a generation of theologians who are well versed in historical and systematic theology—in short, a power in Church and State . . .[9]

Such was Kuyper's reception in America. What was his experience of the country of which he had the impression that his ideals had been realized there as a fruit of Calvinism?

He maintained his enthusiasm for America to the very end of his life. In 1917 we find him declaring: "In America Calvinism has attained its highest development."[10] Yet he was too clear-sighted to overlook entirely certain things which would have become major difficulties if he had had the time and the desire to work them out. But he had no such desire. With all his heart he wished to believe in his dream of America.

There were many aspects of American life that agreed with his original dream. He tells us about them in his charming book of travel impressions entitled *Varia Americana.* In the first chapter of this book he sings the praise of America and the Americans, under the heading "Farther Than Us." America is the land of great freedom, he writes. There each person has an equal chance. The result is that we find in America a class of laborers and farmers who are ahead of the members of the same class in Europe when it comes to their interests and general education:

> Easier circumstances have promoted the development of the lower classes in America in an extraordinary way. Even in rural districts, the workman who reads a newspaper or a magazine is not the exception but an everyday phenomenon. He is abreast of the social and political questions of the day and can talk about them much better than the ordinary citizen who stands behind the counter in The Netherlands.[11]

Kuyper noted that even in rather small cities, the daily newspapers in America were bigger than their European counterparts. Much money was spent on education: "Our richest academy buildings dwindle away when compared with all the halls and chapels and laboratories built in one state for a single university."[12]

The churches were well-built, with excellent seating accommodations. According to Kuyper's figure, the total seating capacity of all the churches in America at that time was about forty-two million, whereas the total population was some sixty-five million. And by his calculations, there were about 112,000 clergymen in the United States.[13]

Religion was held in honor, he said. The sessions of Congress were opened with prayer by a special chaplain. The same was true at Princeton University, where academic affairs were opened in prayer by a Dean.

Many Americans are proud to be the descendents of the first Dutch settlers. Kuyper quoted Judge August Van Wijck, who declared: "If there is a survival of the fittest, we descendents of Dutch extraction interpose the claim that our Dutch element will be permanent and enduring."[14]

In eloquent terms Kuyper described the hardships and energy of the nineteenth-century Dutch settlers in Michigan. He deplored the establishment of the Christian Reformed Church in the following words: "Van Raalte joined the Dutch Reformed Church in 1848, and it is highly deplorable that later all kinds of disputes about Freemasonry and church discipline led to the founding of another group of churches, in addition to and over against the Dutch Reformed." He went on to urge reunion, but then he seemed to hesitate for a moment.

Hesitations

After writing the words quoted above, Kuyper hesitated. Freemasonry—he was an outspoken opponent of this cult! He knew that the Reformed Churches condoned lodge membership, and that the Christian Reformed Churches did not tolerate it. Yet he wanted to bear with those Reformed Churches, which he viewed as the true continuation of the old Calvinistic churches of the seventeenth century. That was why he repeated the words which he must have heard often in Reformed Church circles those days: "American Freemasonry is not as dangerous as the European variety."[15] He had even read in the *New York Tribune* of November 27, 1898, that Freemasonry had been Christianized, according to Christian lodge members.[16]

Now, somewhat reluctantly, his heart and his pen began to protest. He wrote: "Even though we must completely admit that these men were mistaken, that the Christianization of Freemasonry is an illusion, and that the fruit of Freemasonry is *always* opposed to Christianity, it is clear that the cause of this conclusion is only a misunderstanding, and that it is not a conclusion drawn on purpose."[17] And there were other such retractions.

On more than one occasion Kuyper had stressed the richness of the so-called pluriformity of the church. In his Stone Lectures he exclaimed: "After an experience of three centuries it must be confessed that this multiformity, which is inseparably connected with the fundamental thought of Calvinism, has been much more favorable to the growth and prosperity of religious life than the compulsory uniformity in which Rome sought the basis of its strength."[18]

But as he surveyed the American pluriformity, Kuyper lost much of his enthusiasm for it. Although he continued to praise the existence of a number of free churches in a free state, he also became aware that there were many drawbacks to the situation. He saw the danger of competition between churches. One minister would try to outdo the next in his performance in order to attract members to the church. Kuyper offered the following striking example:

> A short time ago there was a church in New York whose morning services were well attended, while the evening services were rather empty. The trustees, convinced that the evening services should be made more attractive, asked the preacher to shorten his sermons and to fill the time with all kinds of choir and solo singing, and also the showing of lantern slides. For some time this proved helpful. But there was no end to these methods, and finally the trustees asked for such a show that the minister refused to cooperate any longer. He protested against the fact that the services were becoming a kind of Sunday *entertainment*, a kind of Sunday *comedy*, and courageously he started preaching again. But the trustees did not agree. He was dismissed.[19]

Kuyper called this a kind of *Pelagianism,* applied to the constitution of a church. (Pelagianism stresses the free will of man; this type of church establishment emphasizes the ingenuity of man—not the engineering of God.)

In the same vein Kuyper criticized the fact that many churches in the United States were money churches and class churches. Generally speaking, he found a good deal of materialism in America.[20] Many of the churches were influenced by such attitudes; in the big cities, especially, one could find separate churches for the rich, the middle class, and the poor. "An elder in such a rich church is like a dead horse tied to a tree," Kuyper wrote.[21] The deacons functioned only at the celebration of the Lord's Supper. In many of the churches there were no catechism classes. There were plenty of Sunday schools, but the lessons lacked biblical substance. Moreover, there was not much knowledge of doctrine in evidence.

Kuyper also noted that the freedom of some seminaries was being curtailed by financiers who pulled the strings. An example was the case of Professor Briggs of Union Seminary in New York. Briggs was suspended from his office by the General Assembly of the Presbyterian Church in 1892 on account of his teachings (he was a vigorous exponent of the higher criticism of the Old Testament), but the directors of Union Seminary, who were men of great financial power, wanted to maintain him and have the Seminary cut its ties with the Presbyterian Church. Briggs would still continue to teach the future ministers of the church.

Kuyper also objected to the Americans' lack of insight into God's covenant and to the needless and endless splitting of American denominations. Despite his many words of appreciation, he could not refrain from saying:

> However much we may try to appreciate American church life, it is an unmistakable fact that some wild branches have developed which should be cut off. The real principles should be studied much more in America. The history of the past should be fundamentally reconstructed.[23]

This was a sweeping judgment, and it could not be applied to each and every church in the United States. But it is clear that although Kuyper still treasured his dream of American liberty, his meeting with the American reality had been something of an eye-opener for him.

Apotheosis of Calvinism

In October of 1898 Kuyper delivered his Stone Lectures on Calvinism in the auditorium of Princeton University.* It was one of the high points of his career. He was sixty-one years old at the time. He had struggled against the waves of the haughty opinions of the modernists of his time and had emerged.** He was an acknowledged leader in church and state. Through his own life's struggle, he had shown that Calvinism was alive and well.

As he spoke, Kuyper stirred the imagination of his audience. He dealt with: "Calvinism as a Life-System," "Calvinism and Religion," "Calvinism and Politics," "Calvinism and Science," "Calvinism and Art," and "Calvinism and the Future." He spoke eloquently and with conviction. He took a broad approach to his subject and to the whole question of the essence of Christianity.

About the same year, the famous Berlin professor Adolf von Harnack delivered his influential lectures on this same topic—the essence of Christianity.[25] Harnack was the man who transposed the essentials of Christianity as we find them in the Apostles' Creed into a modern Humanistic confession about the love of God, who is the Father of all men, and the brotherhood of all men. Kuyper's lectures might be regarded as a counterpoint to Harnack's ideas. He was committed to Calvinism because only Calvinism was able to answer the deepest problems that arose for him when he went astray and could not find rest in any modern system of thought.

What Kuyper was really talking about was *true Christianity*. To him Calvinism was a world-and-life-view; it was the form of religion that started with God and walked with God and ended with God. In his own words:

> It remained the special trait of Calvinism that it placed the believer *before the face of God,* not only in His church, but also in his personal, family, social, and political life. The majesty of God and the authority of God press upon the

---

* He had been invited by the L.P. Stone Lecture Committee. In 1908 Prof. Herman Bavinck delivered the Stone Lectures, taking as his topic "Philosophy of Revelation." The Stone Lectures of 1930 were given by Prof. V. Hepp, who dealt with "Calvinism and Philosophy of Nature."
** This is an allusion to the motto of the Dutch province of Zeeland: "Luctor et emergo."

Calvinist in the whole of his human existence. He is a pilgrim, not in the sense that he is marching through a world with which he has no concern, but in the sense that at every step of the long way he must remember his responsibility to that God so full of majesty, who awaits him at his journey's end.[26]

Harnack stressed the universal love of God and the importance of following Jesus as our example. Kuyper, taking his characteristically Calvinistic approach, emphasized God's eternal predestination and the saving act of Christ on behalf of His own. The people of God are not an aggregate* but are to be viewed as an organic whole:

God so loved the world that He has given Himself to it, in the person of His Son, and thus He has again brought our race, and through our race His whole cosmos, into a renewed contact with eternal life. To be sure, many branches and leaves of the tree of the human race shall fall away, yet the tree itself shall be saved; on its new root in Christ it shall once more blossom gloriously.[27]

Kuyper's lectures contain a profoundly consistent form of God-centered religion. Earlier we saw how he emphasized the necessity of regeneration, of being born again. At two junctures in these lectures, this same emphasis comes through.

In the first of his lectures he compares paganism, Mohammedanism and Roman Catholicism with Calvinism. Paganism tries to find its god(s) in creation, while Mohammendanism isolates God from creation. Roman Catholicism seeks contact with God by means of a mystical connecting link which is to be found in the church. "But only Calvinism proclaims the exalted thought that, although standing in high majesty above the creature, God enters into immediate fellowship with the creatures by means of His Holy Spirit."[28]

At the end of his Stone Lectures, Kuyper returns to that act of the Holy Spirit which is necessary for the achievement of God's purpose with His creatures. As he talks about the future, he portrays his own time in gloomy colors, but then he goes on to compare Calvinism to an Aeolian harp:

---

* Kuyper used this term to stand for loosely connected fragments bunched together.

The period in which we are living at present is surely at a low ebb religiously, and lacks the heroic spark. Unless God sends forth His Spirit, there will be no turn, and fearfully rapid will be the descent of the waters. But you remember the Aeolian harp, which men were wont to place outside their casement, that the breeze might wake its music to life. Until the wind blew, the harp remained silent; on the other hand, even though the wind arose, if the harp did not lie in readiness, not a single note of ethereal music delighted the ear. Now, let Calvinism be nothing but such an Aeolian harp,—absolutely powerless, as it is, without the quickening Spirit of God, still we feel it our God-given duty to keep our harp, its strings turned aright, ready in the window of God's Holy Sion, awaiting the breath of the Spirit.[29]

The six Stone Lectures together constitute a kind of apotheosis of Calvinism, as the most perfect expression of Christianity. As Kuyper put it:

Calvinism first developed a special theology, then a special church order, and then a given form for political and social life, for the relation between nature and grace, between Christianity and the world, between church and state, and finally for art and science, and amid all these expressions of life it remained always the self-same Calvinism, in so far as simultaneously and spontaneously all these developments sprang from its deepest life-principle. Hence to this extent it stands in line with those other great complexes of human life, known as Paganism, Islamism, Romanism and Protestantism, by which we distinguish four entirely different worlds in the one collective world of human life. And if strictly considered you should coordinate Christianity, and not Protestantism, with Paganism and Islamism, it is nevertheless better to place Calvinism in line with them, *because Calvinism claims to embody the Christian idea more purely and accurately than could Romanism and Lutheranism.*

In all his lectures, Kuyper tried to substantiate this claim.

Criticism

The strength and weakness of Kuyper's Stone Lectures on Calvinism lie in their magnificent architecture. In broad outline, Kuyper sketches the lines along which Calvinism has developed —or ought to have developed. But sometimes what he pulls into the grand scheme leads him to say things that are rather bizarre.

Think of his remarkable theory about the "commingling of the blood," mentioned earlier. In order to bolster his thesis that Calvinism is one of the highest phases in the development of the human race, he first states that national isolation leads to degeneration, and that international crossbreeding enhances the quality of human life. He goes on to argue that "the nations among whom Calvinism flourished most widely exhibit in every way this mingling of races." His conclusion is:

> In America, where Calvinism has come to unfold itself in a still higher liberty, this commingling of blood is assuming a larger proportion than has ever yet been known. Here the blood flows together from all the tribes of the ancient world, and again we have the Celts from Ireland, the Germans from Germany and Scandanavia, united to the Slavs from Russia and Poland, who promote still further this already vigorous intermingling of the races. This latter process takes place—in order that the old historic nations are dissolving themselves—to reunite in one higher unity, constantly assimilated by the American type. In this respect Calvinism fully meets the conditions imposed on every new phase of development in the life of humanity. It spread itself in a domain where it found the commingling of blood stronger than under Romanism, and in America raised this up to its highest conceivable realization.[30]

At best these fancy words are an interesting historical speculation, and at worst a dangerous racial theory. But the ideas expressed here are not essential to Kuyper's main argument; they are not repeated in his other works and can be considered a detour made by an energetic mind.

More to the point is the criticism that these Stone Lectures present an idealized picture of Calvinism to which the historic reality did not—and does not—correspond. Kuyper, the architect, loved to build schemes and ideas in a well-ordered manner, according to a systematic plan. But he did not consider the faults and failures of the human reality.*

In his criticism of Kuyper's idea of a Christian culture,[31] A.A. van Ruler often missed the mark, but he was right when he stated that the redemptive work of Christ our Savior became background for Kuyper.[32] As Dr. S.J. Ridderbos put it: "Kuyper did not sufficiently approach the problem of Christian

---

* This criticism applies to the Stone Lectures only. In his other works Kuyper stresses the slogan "Semper reformanda."

culture from the starting-point of justification."[33]

We have spoken about another line of criticism, which accuses Kuyper of "neo-Calvinism." Kuyper's free-church idea and his "pietistic rigorism" are deviations from original Calvinism, according to Troeltsch. But we saw that such criticism is really not justified.

It is most remarkable, however, that Kuyper, near the end of his life, accepted the label "neo-Calvinism" as a legitimate description of his life's work. He defended the position that every current of opinion or school of thought worthy of its name bears the stamp of its time. "This is also true as far as Calvinism is concerned. Calvin himself did not completely fathom or totally work out what was implied in the guiding motive that impelled him."[34]

Kuyper then pointed to the differences in the situation of sixteenth-century Geneva, The Netherlands in the nineteenth century, and the state of affairs in the United States. It was never his desire to be a conservative. He wanted to apply the great principles of Calvinism in his own time, though he was not a modernist. He confessed the same faith as Calvin, and he applied the Calvinistic principles, particularly in the area of politics. What remains important is that he applied them in a way that met the needs of his own time. And in this, he may truly be called a neo-Calvinist.

Chapter 13

The Two Graces

A Shift in Emphasis

After he returned to The Netherlands, Kuyper continued a series of articles in *De Heraut*. He had begun these articles, which dealt with common grace, in September of 1895, and he completed the series in July of 1901.

It should not surprise us that his American lectures manifest the influence of this major study. In his book on Calvinism he pointed repeatedly to the broadness of the Calvinistic worldview. This broadness, he believed, flowed from a recognition of the "grace" of God which is to be observed in all of his creatures and in the entirety of human culture.

On account of this emphasis, Kuyper has often been called the man of common grace. It has been asserted that because Kuyper made much of the goodness of God as still visible in the entire world, he promoted "a process of acute secularization within Christianity."[1]

It cannot be denied that at the time Haitjema made this accusation, secularization had indeed begun to affect large segments of European and American Christianity. The churches in which Kuyper had played a dominant role were not free from its influence. During the first world war, materialism was rampant in many circles. Herman Bavinck wrote the following words of warning: "The strictest orthodoxy cannot cover up the sins of smuggling and usury, of dishonesty and fraud in business, of social and political unrighteousness."[2]

Yet it is most unfair to make Kuyper's doctrine of common grace entirely or even partially responsible for this situation. In fact, we may smile to discover that from the one side he was accused of a "pietistic rigorism," while from the other side he was accused of being an (unintentional) secularist. The truth of the matter, of course, is that he was neither.

In this chapter we will try to determine what Kuyper meant by the term "common grace." But first we must emphasize as strongly as possible that he was as much a man of special grace as of common grace. It may be true that there was a shift in emphasis in a later period of his life, but from the very outset the necessity of God's special grace—acceptance by God as His child apart from any merit on one's own part—was fundamental to Kuyper's thinking. We can safely say that it remained the main concern throughout his life. In short, Kuyper was and remained a Reformed Christian to the end of his life.

Special Grace

Kuyper was convinced that the confession of predestination was the *cor ecclesiae,* the heart of the church.[3] To a certain extent he had learned this from J.H. Scholten, a modernist professor under whom he had studied. Scholten defended the principle of God's absolute sovereignty as the foundation of religion.[4] But after Kuyper's conversion, a conversion in which some inflexible Calvinists were instrumental, he discovered that he differed radically from Scholten. As Kuyper himself tells us, Scholten's modernism was *deterministic,* starting from an *idea* of God, whereas real Reformed theology was *Scriptural,* starting and continuing with the *living God.* A genuinely Reformed theologian should not set up a system, but should listen to the Word, as Mary did at Jesus' feet.[5]

If there is such a thing as predestination, not all men are elected. And if not all are elected, there is a special grace of God, a grace He bestows on His own. It is abundantly evident that the Reformed confessions teach the doctrine of God's special grace. The Heidelberg Catechism clearly declares that not all men will be saved but only those who by faith are ingrafted into Christ and receive all His benefits. And the Canons of Dort state that the fact "that some receive the gift of faith from God, and others do not receive it, proceeds from God's eternal decree."

Yet it was an act of courage on Kuyper's part when he began to proclaim this truth from his pulpit. The years after his installation in Amsterdam, he wrote as follows about this matter:

> Our task was difficult.
>
> For more than 140 years all the prominent and learned theologians in Germany and in our own country had tried with all their skill to contradict, refute and obscure (the doctrine of) special grace. Consequently, in our midst, too, a public opinion had sprung up which branded as foolishness any belief in "particular atonement." Almost all of our Reformed ministers had forgotten that the Reformed church, in its period of flourishing, had always fostered a different view. After all of this, it should not surprise us that some people were rather frightened when, suddenly and unexpectedly, in one of the most widely read church papers, a plea for special grace was announced.
>
> When the author, ten years ago (1879), dared to preach in Amsterdam on "The Comfort of Eternal Election," he occasioned such a sensation in the world of the Amsterdam ministers that shortly afterwards one of his colleagues preached in the Westerkerk (a church in Amsterdam) on the theme "Let Him Who Brings Another Gospel Than That Christ Died for All Men Be Accursed."[6]

It should be noted that here and elsewhere, Kuyper stressed the *comfort* of eternal election. For him predestination was not a cold, hard doctrine to be accepted stoically but was part and parcel of the gospel, the good news. In the sermon referred to, he pleaded with hearers who might be so deeply aware of their sinfulness and unworthiness before God that deep depression might grip their hearts and they might think: "There is no hope for me." He pointed to the words: "But you, O Jacob, whom I have chosen . . . fear not, for I am with you. Be not dismayed, for I am your God. I will strengthen you, I will help you, I will uphold you" (Isaiah 41:8-10).[7]

Kuyper stressed the same point when he discussed predestination at length in his exposition of the Heidelberg Catechism. He pointed to the experience of uncertainty regarding eternal salvation which sometimes weighs down the heart of the believer. "The once so happy man asks himself: Is everything gone now? But then sacred Scripture answers him, and his Savior comforts him with the assurance that divine election is irrevocable, that the seed of God abides in him, and that no one is able to snatch him out of the hand of his Father."[8]

We should not imagine, however, that Kuyper gives his doctrine of special grace a mainly logical or practical foundation. His mainstay is the plain teaching of Scripture! He even dares to write that "there is no Christian church which denies or disputes the fact that Scripture has indeed revealed to us the existence of divine election."[9]

He then goes on to explain the special meaning of the Hebrew term *bachar* and the Greek word *eklegein*.[10] Aware of the fact that the universalists who deny predestination always refer to the same texts (i.e. I John 2:2, I Timothy 2:4, and II Peter 3:9), Kuyper discusses those texts.[11] With regard to I John 2:2 ("And he is an expiation for our sins, and not for ours only, but also for the sins of the whole world"), he makes the following observations. First, the words "the sins of" do not appear in the original text, where we only read: "but also for the whole world." Secondly, the preposition "for" used in the Greek is not "huper" (instead of) but "peri" (in relation to). Thirdly, expiation is not the Greek word for the *means* of reconciliation (as in Romans 3:25), but for the act and fact of reconciliation itself. Fourthly, "the whole world" does not mean all men (see Mark 14:9, 16:15, Romans 1:8, Colossians 1:6, and I John 5:19). In John, "kosmos" means organized life that was overpowered by satan (see I John 2:15, 5:5, etc.). This text speaks first of all of our personal sin, then of the guilt imputed to all the children of Adam, and finally of the work of Christ in behalf of our human race.

As for Christ's work on behalf of the human race, Kuyper maintains strongly that on the one hand Christ bore the wrath of God against the sin of the whole human race and that nothing more would be needed in order to save all the children of man, but on the other hand that Scripture strongly asserts that Jesus died for His own, "whom You have given Me from the world" (John 17:6).[12] He ends his meditations of 1879 with a prayer and a doxology:

> Therefore our soul praises and thanks Thee, O wonderful and all-merciful God, at the end of these meditations.
> We thank Thee that Thou hast esteemed the blood of Thy beloved Son too holy to have it shed while the outcome was

unsure. And that Thou, knowing our ungodly will and the aversion of the imagination of our human heart, didst not leave eternal salvation to the choice of that heart but, breaking through with Thy divine power, didst decide in Thy divine counsel that the blood of Thy dear Son *must* be rewarded. That a congregation of saints *must* appear. And that Thy dear children, whom Thou hast made Thine own and carried over the abyss, would be eternally comforted in a heavenly way by the unchangeability of Thy will.

Forgive, cover, expiate all in the speech of our mouth that was not in accordance with the holiness of Thy house or with the fullness of Thy liberating truth.

By Thy wonderful grace, open the eyes of those who have deviated from Thy truth. Do not hold their sin against them, but enlighten them, that they may be satisfied with seeing Thy likeness (Psalm 17:15).

And if it has been the good pleasure of Thy unsearchable counsel, O Father of all mercies and Source of all salvation, finally to take away the ban which was on our country and our church, and to have mercy on Thy people that returned blushing to Thee, and to breathe the breath of life into the almost dead body of Christ in our country—for Christ's sake, O God, show Thy mercy especially herein, that we learn not to depend on *our* faithfulness, which is nothing, but only and solely on the counsel of Thy will, which commenced, goes on, and will once gloriously finish this precious, good and divine work, to the praise of Thy name! Amen.[13]

Common Grace

Kuyper believed that the grace of God is *one*; it is His undeserved favor toward sinners who are loved with an eternal love and are saved by faith in the blood of Jesus Christ, shed for them. God's grace is not of their own doing but is a divine gift (Ephesians 2:8).

Yet Kuyper has been called the man of common grace. There is no getting around the fact that his teaching was increasingly marked by an emphasis on *two* graces—one for God's elect and the other for all of mankind.

The issue at stake: what did Kuyper mean by common grace? He certainly was not an Arminian. He agreed wholeheartedly with the Canons of Dort in rejecting the error of those

> who teach that the corrupt and natural man can so well use the common grace (by which they understand the light of nature), or the gifts still left him after the fall, that he can gradually gain by their good use a greater, that is, the evangelical or saving grace, and salvation itself. And that in this way God on His part shows Himself ready to reveal Christ unto all men.

Thus there is no saving grace for all men. Yet there is some sort of grace bestowed on all men.

It is an intriguing fact that just when Kuyper began to write on common grace, another great Dutch Reformed theologian tackled the same subject. Herman Bavinck of the seminary in Kampen delivered an address in 1894 on this theme—"De algemeene genade."

This was more than a coincidence. Both Kuyper and Bavinck had studied in Leiden. Bavinck kept his childhood faith, while Kuyper, after a period of some years, rediscovered the treasures of the Reformed faith. To a certain extent, each had enjoyed the Leiden atmosphere; they formed lifelong friendships with some of the gifted men who taught there, despite the fact that they did not hold the same fundamental convictions. They had been confronted with the culture of modern times in its most brilliant representatives. In the course of time they could not help but ask themselves: what is the relation between Christianity and culture? To use ancient Christian terminology, what did Jerusalem have in common with Athens? Or to rephrase the question in terms of the thought of Thomas Aquinas, what was the relation between Augustine's thought and Aristotle's philosophy?

In his address Bavinck pointed to the fact that Calvin appreciated natural life more than the other reformers did.[14] Although the term "common grace" is hardly to be found in his writings,[15] he certainly did teach that after the fall God curtailed the perversity of human nature, preserved human reason, and granted many gifts to all creatures. Calvin pointed to the kindness (*liberalitas*) and benevolence (*benevolentia*) of God as the source of all of this.[16]

Kuyper's treatment of common grace first appeared as a series of weekly articles in *De Heraut* (1895-1901) and was later published as a book in three volumes (1902-05). It became one of his most famous, most disputed and most influential works.[17]

At the outset Kuyper declared that he chose his terminology (i.e. common grace as opposed to general grace) to underscore the fact that he was not talking about saving grace but about the favor God bestowed on all His earthly creatures immediately after the fall into sin. If he had not done so, death and hell would have reigned everywhere. In its definite form, this common grace was proclaimed after the flood in the covenant made with Noah.

Kuyper then went on to explain the difference between the two graces. In the first place, special grace applies to God's elect, whereas common grace applies to mankind in general and to every member of the human race. In the second place, special grace finds its ultimate goal in eternal life, whereas the goal of common grace is the maintenance and development of natural life. And in the third place, special grace results in righteousness before God, whereas common grace results in civil justice.[18]

As far as the development of natural life is concerned, Kuyper pointed to the fact that by common grace the curse is restrained. Although there are thorns and thistles, there is also daily bread. Man is able to continue living; in this sense common grace is the presupposition of human history. God has maintained the conditions and relations of human life.

Kuyper pointed to marriage in its different forms, some of which are totally corrupted. And yet, despite the corruptions, marriage is a source of blessing. He spoke in a similar way of family life, of all societal relations, and of the totality of humanity.

Until the building of the tower of Babel, mankind was an organic unity, but after the confusion of the languages separate states originated. The state as such is a gift of God. The mere fact that there are governments produces a certain restraint of the effects of sin. In summary, it is because of God's common grace that it is still possible to live in this world. To a certain extent, the potentials of the original creation can still be realized.

To a certain extent—Kuyper did expect that higher culture would deteriorate. (By higher culture he meant such things as the recognition of God and respect for the good, the true and the beautiful.) Yet he expected things to improve in the area of technical culture, in man's increasing mastery of the powers of nature.

Thus we see that common grace serves both the coming of the kingdom of God and the coming of the Antichrist. By conserving humanity it prepares a place for the gospel, but it also serves as a foundation for the development of sin, which will culminate in the appearance of the man of sin.

Kuyper's doctrine of common grace proved very influential, for it led to a reconsideration of the relation of Christianity to general human culture. There had been an anti-cultural streak in the rather small group of nineteenth-century Dutch Reformed Christians. These people had taken on the role of second class citizens who had to walk along the side of the road rather than in the middle. They had generally been wary of modern inventions and associations that seemed to conflict with an attitude of humble godliness. For example, many of them had condemned vaccination against smallpox on the grounds that it represented tampering with the human body and manifested a lack of faith in God's providence. They also had objections to fire insurance and life insurance: a believer should trust in the Lord and leave the future completely in His hands.

In his lengthy discussion of common grace Kuyper discussed these problems in detail.[19] He showed from the Bible that taking precautions was a gift of God, even a divine command.

Aftermath

Kuyper's doctrine of common grace did not go unchallenged. On the one hand there were many people who enjoyed his treatment of the subject and declared that their whole outlook on life had been broadened by it.[20] On the other hand, debates about the doctrine of common grace soon sprang up in Kuyper's own circles. Some of the theologians of the Dutch Reformed Church (*Nederlandse Hervormde Kerk*) expressed their disagreement, and the doctrine occasioned a schism even in the Christian Reformed Church of North America.

In Kuyper's own circles the following questions were raised. Is the source of common grace to be found in Christ as the Mediator of creation, the true light that enlightens every man? (John 1:9). This was indeed what Kuyper taught. Or should common grace be ascribed to Christ as the Mediator of redemption, as men like S.G. De Graaf and Herman Dooyeweerd maintained? Another question was whether common grace had a purpose of its own, such as the development of the potentials of creation. If not, was it extended to men only for the sake of special grace?

These questions were discussed mainly after Kuyper's death. Criticisms were also advanced by the Dutch Reformed (*Hervormd*) theologians T.L. Haitjema and A.A. van Ruler. Both these men, who were proponents of the idea of a national church, opposed Kuyper's doctrine of special grace for the elect only. Van Ruler branded this doctrine spiritualistic and dualistic; he preferred to speak of the one grace of Jesus Christ, which is the source of the renewal of human life in its totality.[21]

At about the same time the Kampen theologian Klaas Schilder criticized Kuyper's view of common grace sharply. Schilder did not want to use the term "grace" in reference to unbelievers, for God is not gracious to them. Taking his point of departure in the covenant of works established by God in Paradise, Schilder proposed to speak instead of a common *obligation* (to keep the covenant) or a common *mandate* (to till and keep the earth). After the fall God maintains the laws of nature. Although he preserves the world and leads it to its consummation, this activity on His part cannot be called grace. Rather, the Lord Jesus loves His creation, but He is angry with the wicked. Hence we can speak of common judgment.[22]

Disputes and arguments about common grace gave rise to a good deal of friction. In 1942, the synod of the Reformed Churches of The Netherlands finally issued the following doctrinal decision:

> The church confesses:
> 1. That immediately after the fall God began to gather His church, which He delivers from sin, death, and the curse. Yet even though His wrath is revealed against all ungodliness and wickedness of men (Romans 1:18), He does not inflict the complete punishment for sin upon the fallen world during this dispensation; rather, while enduring her in His patience, He makes His sun to rise on the evil and on the good, and does good from heaven to all mankind (Matthew 5:45; Acts 14:17).
> 2. That He still left in man some small remnant of the original gifts of creation and some light of nature, even if all of this is quite insufficient for salvation, and even if man, in things natural and civil, does not use this light properly (Belgic Confession, Article 14; Canons of Dort, III and IV, 4).

3. That these remains and benefits serve not only to take all excuse away from man but also to check sin temporarily in its growth, so that possibilities given in the original creation are still able to be developed in this sinful world.

4. That God herein shows His sovereign goodness to the evil and the good, the just and the unjust, indicated among us by means of the term "general grace" or "common grace," which grace is to be distinguished clearly from the saving grace given to those who have been given by the Father to Christ.[23]

After this decision was made, the debates started again, and two years later there was a rupture in the church. What must be stressed, however, is that in 1942 there was unanimity in the Reformed Churches of The Netherlands with regard to the common grace issue, and that this unanimity was in line with Kuyper's insights.

In the Christian Reformed Churches of North America there were also protests against Kuyper's position on common grace. In his lectures on Calvinism he had declared that "God, maintaining the life of the world, relaxes the curse which rests upon it, arrests its process of corruption, and thus allows the untrammeled development of our life in which to glorify Himself as creator."[24] H. Hoeksema and H. Danhof, two ministers in the Christian Reformed Church, were convinced that only God's elect are the recipients of His grace. Strictly speaking, then, not even a well-meant offer of grace could be extended to all men. Moreover, they were convinced that the introduction of a "common grace" would promote worldliness.

At their synod of 1942, meeting in Kalamazoo, the Christian Reformed Churches made a decision with regard to the common grace controversy. The report that had been prepared for synod quoted a number of classic Reformed theologians, such as Calvin, Ursinus and Mastricht. The conclusion reached by the synod was that there is indeed a certain favor or grace of God which He shows to all of His creatures, that there is a restraint of sin, and that the unregenerate, although incapable of any *saving* good, can perform *civic* good. The same synod issued a serious testimony to the churches in which it warned against the dangers of worldliness.[25]

Despite these efforts, there was also a rupture in the Christian Reformed Church. Those who did not agree with the "three points of Kalamazoo" formed a new denomination—the Protestant Reformed Church.

Chapter 14

Christic Our King

Kuyper's Heart

Abraham Kuyper was a child of God—this is by far the finest thing that can be said about him. His heart was with his God, and his heart was also with the people of God. It has been pointed out by a number of observers that he was a *mystical* man.

Now the word "mystical" has more than one meaning. Generally speaking, it stands for the experience of personal contact with God. It might refer to that contact as an effect of the Holy Spirit's work in the human heart and as a response to God's inspired Word. It has also been taken to mean an immediate contact with the divine world. Such mysticism is found not only in Christianity but also in Buddhism, Hinduism, Islam, and other religions.

Kuyper warned against what he called "*false* mysticism." He wrote about "mystically inclined souls who want to go their own way and fall repeatedly into all sorts of heresy and even into moral errors of various kinds."[1] But he loved to speak of the mystical union of his own heart, and of the heart of all God's children, with Christ.

This was so much a part of his lifestyle that after his death he was remembered for it above all other things. His close friend Idenburg spoke at his funeral. He had visited Kuyper daily during the long period of his sickness, and he referred to his friend's tenderheartedness:

> This tenderness in the depths of his soul was a great love, which in the first place went out toward God, the God of his

145

life. How his eyes could sparkle and his words glow when he talked confidentially about the experiences of his life and the way the Lord had guided him! It was that love which made him witness, even on his deathbed, that God was his refuge and his strength, a very present help in trouble.

He revealed that tenderness of his soul most clearly in his meditations. How deeply he experienced the blessedness of "being near to God."[2]

The Amsterdam minister V. Hepp, who in 1922 became Herman Bavinck's successor at the Free University, drew attention to Kuyper's meditations when speaking at his funeral. He paid lavish tribute to Kuyper's intellect, his logical reasoning, his will-power, his organizational talent, and the great results of these qualities. But then he went on to say:

> Yet he would not have been able to achieve all of this if there had not been a strong mystical relationship between him and the people who loved the Reformed confession. He did not conceal that relationship but spoke about it publicly. Kuyper was a mystic figure who can be compared with Augustine, Thomas à Kempis and Pascal. Through his mysticism he enjoyed the confidence of the many who loved the Reformed truth.[3]

In his meditations, Kuyper opened his heart. For years he wrote one every Sunday afternoon. They were so much a part of his life that even when he was prime minister of The Netherlands he continued this devout Sunday labor. He talked with his people, he talked with himself, and he talked with his God.

A striking example of the way in which Kuyper meditated is to be found in *De Heraut* of September 3, 1899. That week Kuyper's wife had died, in Meyringen (Switzerland), where they had intended to enjoy a holiday. Kuyper was at her side when she died, and he wrote his weekly meditation on II Corinthians 5:4: "That what is mortal may be swallowed up by life." He started with the following words:

> When you are at a deathbed, your eyes seem to tell you only that Death, that terrible enemy of God and men, has finally succeeded in devouring a life that is very dear to you.
>
> It was not his first attack. It is most exceptional when someone dies who has not been ill before and has never been faced with the terror of death.
>
> But those former attacks of death did not succeed. After weeping in the evening there was joy in the morning. And oh,

what an inexpressible comfort it was for the heart to receive back our dear sick ones! But now everything was different.

Nothing helped, nothing availed any more. And when the sick one gave up the ghost, it seemed that Death, after all one's unheard prayers and meaningless cares, laughed and whispered mockingly: "I have won, and the morning of your joy has not come . . . That is reality . . ."

You have prayed—and God did *not* answer. And you know that death is caused by sin. And you tremble before His holiness. But talking about God's love, when He allows the one who was dearest to you on earth to be snatched from your side . . .

That was the beginning of this meditation, which came straight from Kuyper's heart and must have touched the hearts of his readers. But from there he went on to write the words:

But now comes the Word of God, and that Word, without taking anything away from the hard realities, reverses everything.

It does so totally and completely.

As far as our physical eye is concerned, things are still the same. But there is also an eye of the soul, an eye that remains stoneblind and sees *nothing* until God converts you and *makes* you see spiritually.

And then, before your soul's eye, another reality appears, a *totally reversed* reality. You now see that Death does not devour life but that, in dying, *what is mortal is swallowed up by life.*

How is this possible? No one is able to solve this puzzle. But it happens, and it is true, *in Jesus*, in that Wonderful One who Himself wrestled with Death and forced him to admit Him to glory, opening a way behind Himself in order to bring it about that Death should become instrumental in admitting all who belong to Him to glory.

Still further we read these tender words:

It is not that your beloved dies here, while Jesus is at a far distance, and the one who dies then goes to Him. No, He is present. He did it. And when Death grimaced at you as if he had conquered, your Savior smiled at you and showed you the crown, the palm of victory.[4]

What was Kuyper aiming at when he opened his heart in his meditations? Together with all the people of God, he wanted to live in the fear of the Lord. By this he meant living with Him and for Him, and in all things endeavoring to please Him. He wanted to be *near to God*. He meditated on this expression from Psalm 73 in the following words:

> *Near* is close to God, so that your eye sees Him, your heart becomes aware of Him, your ear hears Him, and all that keeps you separate has disappeared. *Near* is one of the two: either you feel as if caught up in the heavens, or your God has descended from those heavens to visit you where you are, in your loneliness, in your cross, or in the joys of your life that you received. That "near" tells you that there is so very much that separates you from your God, so much by which you stand on your own and feel lonely and desolate, because God went away from you or you went away from God. But it also tells you that you are uneasy with it, that you cannot stand it, that at such a time all that is within you looks out for Him, until that which caused the separation has passed away. And then the meeting is there again. He is again *near* you, and you know again that you are *near* God.[5]

This was indeed a deep mysticism, and Kuyper was aware of the danger involved. "It is a dangerous thing to descend into the depths of mysticism. The soul that seeks God tends almost impulsively to overstep the bounds included in being 'near' God and tries to penetrate into the essence of God." Kuyper adds, however, that an intellectual religion lacks the living water, and that we find a wholesome emphasis on personal contact with God in the church fathers and the Reformers.* He concludes with the following words:

> Affirmation of the right confession, without drinking from the waters, degenerates into dead orthodoxy, just as much as trembling tenderness without a clear confession plunges into the morass of unhealthy mysticism. Only one who feels, searches, and knows he has personal contact with the living God, and in doing so always subjects his spiritual experience to the Word, stands on safe ground, manifests power, and maintains, as far as he is concerned, the power of religion in his house, in his circle, among our people, such a one inspires reverence even among those who despise God and His Word.[6]

---

* He singles out John Calvin, of whom he writes: "Calvin is called cold, but there is no theologian who placed greater emphasis on the mystical union with Christ, and in Him with the Eternal One."

What Christ Did

In the words quoted above, Kuyper mentioned "the power of religion." He was a powerful religious figure as he spoke, activated, and organized the people of God. Yet, in the midst of all he did, he was keenly aware that he could not open the door of heaven even an inch. He knew that the foundation and factuality and finish of our righteousness before God are to be found only in the One who said, once and for all: "It is finished."

It is noteworthy, therefore, that in his 1891 speech on the social problem, Kuyper speaks of the *cruelty* of the socialists who claim to use their power to improve working conditions, when in fact they at the same time take away "the hope for an everlasting glory."[7] Why does Kuyper speak here of cruelty? Jesus indeed had mercy on the poor and we are called to do social justice in His name, but His work was essentially *not* that of a social reformer; rather, it was the work of the *Savior of the world*. Jesus opened the door of the Kingdom of heaven. Elsewhere Kuyper states: "Our definite disagreement with the socialists is that they don't hold out a hand to save people from eternal destruction, while we, the Calvinists, as confessors of the Christ, struggle against social injustice only in connection with the Kingdom of heaven."[8] Christ has brought us back to God, once and for all!

This is the underlying motive of all of Kuyper's work. When he deals at length with the sixteenth Lord's Day of the Heidelberg Catechism, which talks about the suffering and death of our Savior, he points out that when Jesus did everything for us, it was not just through his passive obedience but also through his active obedience. Then, all of a sudden he tells us which answer in the Catechism he finds the most beautiful of all.[9] It comes in another Lord's Day, the twenty-third, where we read:

> How are you righteous before God? Only by a true faith in Jesus Christ; that is, though my conscience accuse me that I have grievously sinned against all the commandments of God and kept none of them, and am still inclined toward all evil, yet God, without any merit of mine, of mere grace, grants and imputes to me the perfect satisfaction, righteousness and holiness of Christ, as if I had never committed any sin, and

myself had accomplished all the obedience which Christ has rendered for me; if only I accept such benefit with a believing heart.

This was the fundamental confession of the Reformation. Kuyper wanted to maintain the purity of that confession in his own time—not just over against the socialists with their secularized messianic ideals, but also in the face of the modernists and the middle-of-the-road theologians who either praised Christ as a kind of ideal man or, confessing His divinity, still did not look up to Him as the Redeemer who bought them with the price of His blood.

In *De Vleeschwording des Woords*, his monograph of 1887 dealing with the incarnation, Kuyper demonstrates the fallacy behind the idea that Christ would have become man even if there had been no fall into sin. First of all he brands this idea, which was espoused by several theologians of his time, an idle speculation invented by Origen. He also calls it an opinion in conflict with Scripture, which speaks to us of no other incarnation than the one on behalf of sinners.[10] Sinners need a mediator. When their eyes are opened to their guilt and their helplessness in the face of the holiness of God, they find in the Gospels the One who carried away their sin from the moment of His incarnation to His death on the cross.[11]

It is impossible, therefore, to write a "life of Jesus." In the course of the nineteenth century a number of lives of Jesus were attempted. The best known of them were by Strauss and Renan. Such books offered their readers a biography of Jesus. But Kuyper asks: How can you write a biography of a man whose life was a constant dying, a constant dying in the place of sinners? How can you write a biography of the Mediator who humiliated Himself for us, being the eternal Son of God?[12]

Christ is our only Savior. We should not honor His eminent human personality; we should honor the Son of God, who is given to us as the Lamb of God who took away the sin of the world.

What Christ Does

Even today, Christ lives for us and works for us. When He was raised from the dead, it was clear that He had finished all that had to be done for sinners. But now He continues "to make us partakers of the righteousness He has obtained for us by His death." Therefore He lives to pray for us[13] and to apply what He has done by the gift of His Holy Spirit.

Kuyper devoted one of his voluminous works to the operation of the Holy Spirit.[14] In this work we encounter wonderful passages about the love of God. However, it is when Kuyper develops his ideas about *Christ's lordship over the world's history* that we find the distinctive Kuyperian stamp. He distinguishes four periods in Christ's Kingship. The first is that of *preparation* (Adam to John the Baptist), the second that of *foundation* (Bethlehem to the ascension), the third that of *extension* (the history of the church connected with that of the world), and the fourth that of *consummation* (after Christ's return).[15] With regard to the third period Kuyper states:

> The course of history and the march of events in all areas of life are important factors in making the nations accessible or inaccessible to Jesus. Moreover, the history of the church on this earth is continuously influenced by all sorts of external events, so that there are entire regions (e.g. in Asia Minor and in North Africa) where the church prospered at one time but afterward, through a series of events, totally disappeared. Because of these facts, it must be the case that the future of the Church, and also that of the heavenly kingdom, could only be guaranteed by a King who has dominion not only in spiritual affairs but also in all the events that decide the destiny of nations. We cannot isolate the course of spiritual affairs from the course of earthly events; that would be a false spiritualism, which is contradicted by the entire course of history.[16]

Christ reigns over history in its totality in order to open the door for the coming of the Kingdom of God. Kuyper stresses that in this period of extension Christ usually makes use of ordinary (as opposed to miraculous) means. The earlier periods were marked by a number of miracles, but the period we now live in does not manifest a constantly miraculous power. What we see is instead the working of "the leaven which a woman took and hid in three measures of flour until it was all leavened."[17]

Christ's dominion extends to the four areas of the human *soul*, the human *body*, man's *contact with others,* and his being *tempted* by the evil one. As for the soul, the act of regeneration is, and always remains, a miracle; yet the miracle is ordinarily embedded in God's covenantal grace and is supported by the ministry of the church. As far as the human body and also the entire realm of nature is concerned, medical science has developed particularly under Christian influence. The opening of the storehouse of nature continues. As for human society in its broadest extent, the reign of Christ did not bring revolution but renewal; it promoted the general welfare. Finally, the anti-demonic action of Jesus Christ has changed the character of formerly pagan countries. Although the power of satan is still strong and in some places is even increasing, the *spirit of the times* has been mightily influenced by Christian motives.[18]

Let Christ Be King

It is Christ who brings all things to their consummation. In the meantime, Christians are called to honor Him as their King. In which way should they do so? Kuyper does not expect them to establish a totally new state of affairs. "The name 'Christian' does not entail all sorts of new inventions and the setting up of a new creation; rather, it entails returning to the old creation and building on the old foundation, and at the same time combatting sin and trusting in Christ's redemption."[19]

Combatting sin and trusting in Christ's redemption—this is the task of the Christian, the task to which he is called in his personal life, in the church, in family life, in society, in the state, and in the realms of science and art. In *Pro Rege* Kuyper gives us a masterful treatment of this idea of the vocation of the Christian in all of these areas of life. He demonstrates a thorough knowledge of history, opens brilliant perspectives, and adds a special Kuyperian touch in the way he deals with practical details.

One such detail is what he has to say about *politeness* as he writes about the practical life of the Christian. He reminds us that the apostle Paul admonished his readers "to be not quarrelsome but kindly to everyone" (II Timothy 2:24). Paul also wrote that he was gentle among those who had hurt him (I Thessalonians 2:7). Kuyper adds:

> Always judging others and always trying to express by a surly face and a grim word how you size up another person—this is not as it ought to be. Our God did not give us the mobile features of our face and the expressiveness of our eyes for us to express our morosity. We should laugh more.[20]

Another such detail is his exposition of the value of playing games. Kuyper tells us that the animals play and that God's angels play before His holy throne. We should do the same, for our human nature needs relaxation.[21] Kuyper had written about this matter before and had shown in his lectures on Calvinism that Calvinists were opposed to card-playing, theater and dancing.[22]

In *Pro Rege* he demonstrates an almost baffling knowledge of all sorts of games. Then he offers some qualifications. After stressing that the nature of a game is perverted when the lust for money starts to play a role, Kuyper continues:

> In itself, of course, card-playing is as innocent as any other game, being stimulated partly by skill and partly by good luck. Yet its abuse by our people rightly condemned it. Sin had a similar effect, although in a different manner, by combining some games with *immorality*. This was mainly the case with respect to the dance and comedy. Both are innocent in themselves. We like to see children hopping, jumping and dancing, and we enjoy their little comedies. But when they get older, passions get the upper hand and cause the character of innocence to disappear. This is most clear as far as dancing is concerned, and our theater was also totally corrupted by it. Calvin allowed popular plays to be performed on the public square. No harm was done when a historical drama or a morality play was performed by living persons. But gradually comedy became the stage of professional artists, and when women finally began to participate in a shameless manner, theater degenerated into an exhibition of immorality and sin. A virtuous play was not attractive, but a dirty play made piles of money. That was the reason why our theater deteriorated totally.[23]

I mention these details to show that Kuyper was not indulging in abstract reasoning; rather, he used every opportunity to apply his line of thought to the practice of the Christian life. He constantly urged his fellow Christians to *glorify their King in all areas of life.* Apart from the institutional church, he spoke of three areas in which they should show their colors. The first was *Christian family life.* Closely connected with it, of course, was the Christian school and the promotion of Christian instruction.

The second area was *Christian organizations.* According to Kuyper, the fundamental idea behind Christian organizations goes all the way back to the apostolic injunction that believers are not to take their grievances to a worldly judge and are not to be mismated with unbelievers (see I Corinthians 6:1-6; II Corinthians 6:14). As for the situation in Kuyper's days in The Netherlands, even in so-called neutral organizations, the leadership was usually in the hands of unbelievers. The watchword of a good organization should be: "Let Christ be King!" "Everyone must make up his mind whether he will become a member of Christian organizations or worldly organizations. This choice is a life-choice."[24]

The third area is that of the *press* or, to use a broader term, the media. To a considerable extent, public opinion is molded by the press. For a long time Christians have stood on the sidelines and have not actively participated, but times have changed, Kuyper said. "The weapons used against us are now taken up by us. Our King does not allow and tolerate a situation in which this armor remains exclusively in the hands of those who represent the spirit of the world."[25] Kuyper himself was a living example of the great potential influence of a Christian newspaper and in general, of Christian literature.

Kuyper went on to write about the necessity of serving Christ in the realms of *science* and *the arts.* He used beautiful words to disclose the deepest motives of the Christian scientist:

> The final goal of the Christian scientist is neither some abstract knowledge nor a multitude of knowledge nor finding a mirror of our own selfhood in the world around us. The Christian scientist does not find rest until he has met the living God Himself. He wants to come face to face with the One who does not *have* wisdom but *is* wisdom, who causes all things to be, upholds them, and contemplates them. No man, no prophet, no angel can give that to us. It can only be given by the One who could say: I and the Father are one.[26]

Relation to Common Grace

There is one final question that we cannot help but ask here: How is Kuyper's doctrine of common grace related to his conception of the kingship of Christ? He had described the action of common grace as the keeping and developing of the powers and possibilities of the original creation, and also as the precondition for the operation of special grace. But did he also picture the kingship of Christ extending over the entire creation of God? Do we find an overlap here, or at least some analogy between similar ideas?

Kuyper himself suggested an answer to this question at the end of *Pro Rege*. He pointed out that for many years the confession that Christ is our High Priest had been not just the central confession of believers but their exclusive confession. His kingship had been nominally accepted but was practically neglected. Consequently, the life and history of the nations had come to be viewed as a product of the human mind. This was the reason why

> I had made an effort, in my three-volume work *Common Grace,* to draw a systematic picture of the meaning of the work of God in the life of the nations and in society-without-Christ. But this was not the end of my investigation. Too often believers imagined that until the day of Christ's return, two separate parts of our human race would exist, the one part to be found in the society of Christians, and the other part in society outside Christianity. Furthermore, such believers suppose that Christ reigns as King over the Christian segment of the population but exerts no influence on the other segment. Therefore *Pro Rege* had to be written as a sequel to *Common Grace*. In *Common Grace* it was demonstrated that all that was beautiful and noble in the life of the nations before and after Christ's coming was solely due to the grace of God, who had been merciful to the nations. The purpose of *Pro Rege,* however, was to demonstrate how the kingship of Christ also dominates the total course of human life.[27]

Kuyper adds a very relevant warning, namely, that we should be *personally* aware that Christ is *our* King.

Chapter 15

On the Sidelines

Blocked in Mid-Career

During the course of his political career, Kuyper more than once used the term *antithesis*. In 1918 he gave the following explanation of this term: "It is a mystery not to be fathomed, but I am only stating a fact when I say that, apart from denominational differences, it seems that about half of the population in any (Christian) country is either inclined to honor Christ our King or to dishonor Him."[1]

Kuyper personally experienced the fierceness of the antithesis in 1905, when his government was brought down by an opposition campaign that has often been characterized as a smear campaign. At first the results of that election seemed to support Kuyper. The parties that supported Kuyper's cabinet received 332,762 votes on the first ballot, while the opposition parties received 283,907 votes.[2] However, the seats in the House of Commons were apportioned on the basis of the various districts into which the country was divided. In some of those districts a second ballot was deemed necessary, and the final result was that the "left" wound up with fifty-two seats, while the "right" won only forty-eight.

The liberals, who were often divided among themselves, formed a united front against Kuyper, for he had disturbed their dream of a national church and a national school. Moreover, he had put an end to their monopoly on the appointment of mayors, notaries and other officials. One of the most able liberal journalists wrote: "Kuyper is the great danger—Kuyper and his Calvinist birds of prey who hover and spy over the fields of The

Netherlands, over the public schools, over the public positions, over the university and the courtroom, over all of national life."[3]

The Social Democrats hated Kuyper with a perfect hatred. They could not forget for a moment that he had thwarted their efforts to seize the reins of government by means of a general strike, and that he had branded their strike a "criminal agitation." In their daily newspaper *Het Volk* (The People), one of them wrote that "in order to keep Kuyper out, one should prefer, if need be, to vote for the devil."[4] The opposition stooped so low that A.E.J. Holwerda, a professor at Leiden, felt impelled to write a brochure entitled "Can't We Change?" He declared: "Only rarely has an opposition in our country been so mean and so petty as the opposition arrayed against Dr. Kuyper."

Now, Kuyper would have had to be superhuman not to feel these blows. Yet, he was already somewhat accustomed to this sort of thing, for in the days of the Doleantie he had also been vilified and abused. However, there were two things that hurt him more than words could express.

The first one was the widespread failure to understand that all of his governmental and parliamentary activities had been part and parcel of a great dream. His labors had not been devoted to achieving an antithesis; it was not his aim to divide the country into two camps. He had struggled for the "pro rege" ideal, and his wholehearted desire was that the majority of his countrymen would turn to God. For this reason he yearned to complete his legislative activities, particularly in the areas of social life and education. But for the time being, at least, the dream would not be realized.

Kuyper was even more frustrated by the fact that his leadership was called into question by some of his own party members. Certain of the so-called Christian Democrats criticized Kuyper constantly and contributed to his downfall, remaining in the Anti-Revolutionary Party all the while. Kuyper was more and more frustrated by certain forms of opposition and by the lack of cooperation in his own ranks. Things went so far that at the 1908 annual meeting of the delegates to his party he prayed that it might please God to ward off the "demonic power" that was trying to disrupt the unity of the brothers.[5]

Was it really as bad as that? We should not be too hasty in our judgment. Doubtless it pleases the prince of darkness to see brothers fighting and throwing accusations at each other. The apostolic warning should always be heeded: "Give no opportunity to the devil" (Ephesians 4:27). We should not refer to the devil, however, as long as there are human factors in the picture that might explain the situation.

There certainly were some human factors that could be mentioned. In the first place, Kuyper has been called "the bell-ringer of the little men."[6] There is some truth to this characterization, for through his incessant labors he did achieve the *emancipation* of the "little man." It might be expected that his followers would be extremely thankful to him—and they were. His opponents often said that he was idolized by his adherents.

Yet there was another side to this coin. Kuyper had educated his people and had opened new perspectives for them in many ways. Still, it should not surprise us that a number of them were not content merely to repeat his words but wanted to rethink his approach—often in a somewhat independent manner. Kuyper had founded his university, and it was small wonder that among the professors of that academy some men were found who in some respects differed from his opinions.

In 1908, a Free University professor named P.D. Fabius wrote a brochure directed against some of Kuyper's ideas, especially his proposal regarding compulsory workman's insurance. That same year Theo Heemskerk, who was Kuyper's friend and a member of the Anti-Revolutionary Party, became prime minister. Heemskerk's father had been a conservative prime minister during the 1860s, but the younger Heemskerk sided with Kuyper, to whom he had written in 1881: "Once, in my student years, I showed myself to be of a different spirit than yours . . . But at a critical moment of my life I came to know divine redemption through the cross of Christ, and from that starting point my convictions concerning constitutional and political questions became Reformed."[7]

Heemskerk had been an influential Anti-Revolutionary member of parliament since 1888, and in 1908 he was appointed prime minister. Kuyper resented the fact that Heemskerk accepted the appointment. He had himself been out of parliament since 1905, but he still hoped for a new chance to become prime minister in 1909, which would give him the opportunity to complete his reform program.

Although the Heemskerk cabinet worked in Kuyper's line and had been hailed by Kuyper in 1908 as a *strong* cabinet,[8] it double-crossed his expectations in certain ways. From this time forward, Kuyper's place was on the sidelines. He occupied this position with as much grace as possible, and he supported the new cabinet in *De Standaard,* but it is unmistakable that he was sometimes reluctant about it.

He remained the trusted leader of his party, acclaimed by the rank-and-file members. Yet there were occasional rumblings from among the trained intellectuals who shared his fundamental convictions but differed here or there on the practical applications, or perhaps did not like the pontifical manner, as they saw it, in which Kuyper sometimes addressed the electorate.

The latest conflict came into the open in 1915, when Kuyper was seventy-eight years old. It was a bitter pill for the old leader to swallow, for that year no fewer than three brochures were written against his leadership. The authors of these brochures were men who, despite the conflict, were actually quite close and dear to Kuyper.

The first of these brochures was written by Koffyberg, a Reformed minister who criticized Kuyper's pro-German sentiments during World War I. It was indeed a fact that, ever since the Boer War, Kuyper did not trust the English but sympathized to a considerable extent with the German emperor.[9] The second brochure was written by Heemskerk. It was an apologia written to counter Kuyper's accusation that Heemskerk had conspired against him.

The third brochure was written by a number of men who ranked among the ten most important people in the Anti-Revolutionary Party—the professors A. Anema, H. Bavinck, and P.A. Diepenhorst, and the politicians Theo Heemskerk and S. De Vries. The brochure was entitled "Leader and Leadership in the Anti-Revolutionary Party." Its main thrust was that it was time for Kuyper to realize that the party he had organized had changed. The period of naiveté was over. There should be more room for open discussion at the party meetings; in particular, the intellectuals should have more opportunity to express their views.

This brochure was not well received. A number of Kuyper's most faithful friends came to his defense. J.C. Sikkel, an impulsive Doleantie minister, had already written the following beautiful words about Kuyper in 1912:

> We are not servants of Kuyper, and we never will be. But we love him so much! And we are so thankful to him! We will always be faithful to him. He was—and still is—so much to us; he meant so very much for us in our conscious and dedicated Christian life, in our Christian communion in all areas of life. In fact, even now, in spite of all our Christian men and powers, we do not feel safe without Dr. Kuyper and *De Standaard* watching over us.[10]

Even more beautiful was the fact that Dr. Kuyper and his Anti-Revolutionary opponents were always aware that at bottom they agreed. In 1913 Kuyper called the Heemskerk cabinet "a picked body of men, more talented than even the best cabinet in the days of the great liberal leader Thorbecke."[11] A year before his death, Kuyper admitted that he had been wrong in suspecting Heemskerk of engaging in intrigues back in 1907.[12]

Around the Ancient World Sea

From November of 1906 to October of 1908, Kuyper traveled through the Levant. He published an account of this journey, interspersed with discussions of current issues, in a two-volume work entitled *Om de oude wereldzee* (Around the Ancient World Sea). Apparently he had needed a break. He expected that the animosity against him would cool off during his absence. Moreover, for a long time he had cherished the hope of visiting the Holy Land. After a visit to the garden of Gethsemane, he sent an olive branch to the queen of The Netherlands, noting that the branch had been taken from one of the trees that had stood in this garden since the day "when our Savior, in this garden, wrestled against pains heavier than death itself." The queen responded with appropriate thanks to his gift and eloquent words.

In this book Kuyper demonstrated the breadth of his vision and the wide-ranging character of his thought. He was especially struck by the resurgence of Islam. In *Pro Rege*, a later, more important work to which I referred earlier, Kuyper begins by comparing Christ and Mohammed. He was deeply impressed by the faithfulness of the Muslims to their prophet. Even the modernized, liberal Muslims do not want to hear a word of criticism directed against their prophet. Kuyper's hope in making this point was that those who called themselves Christians would be shamed into standing up for Christ as their king with equal zeal.

Among the problems Kuyper discussed in *Om de oude wereldzee* was what he called "the Asiatic danger." He dealt with the resurgence of Islam in relation to this problem. Europe had exploited Asia economically and subjected her politically. To these developments there would inevitably be a reaction. Kuyper was convinced that in the course of time Japan would join forces with Islam.

He also wrote about the Russian "soul." Ever since the theological struggle over the *filioque* clause, the Russians have tended toward mysticism. Their mysticism expresses itself in the form of passivity, but also in unreasonable activity, in the expectation of sudden, miraculous changes, perhaps by means of nihilism or terrorism.

One of the main problems he discussed was that of the Jews. In an earlier brochure about the Jews (*Liberalisten en Joden,* 1878) he had exposed the undue influence of the Jews in the financial world and the press and had compared the modern theologians to the Reform Jews, who were in the grip of the same spirit of apostasy. On the other hand, he had also noted in this brochure that Israel was a people that "still had an eminent significance for the future of the kingdom of God."

In *Om de oude wereldzee* Kuyper began his exposition of the Jewish problem with the words: "Israel, among the nations, is and remains a miracle of God's providence to all who believe in the prophecies—and an insoluble enigma to all who reject the prophecies."[13] There is still a Jewish people, a Jewish nationality, Kuyper noted, but there is also a rising tide of anti-Semitism and a growing Zionist movement. Kuyper discussed the causes of anti-Semitism. On the one hand he noted the existence of racism, and on the other hand he spoke of the intellectual and financial power of the Jews, many of whom had abandoned the religion of their fathers. "It is still always a people second to none, but the gold of its original prominence is darkened, so that all that glittered in those mighty spirits—Spinoza, Marx, Heine—did not grow out of the root of Israel but out of the spirit of the surrounding nations.''

As far as the pogroms were concerned, Kuyper pointed out that the Jews were often made the scapegoat when things went wrong in Russia, e.g. after the murder of Czar Alexander II. On the other hand, the Jews had often served as agents of the government in its oppression of the people. The pogroms were a disgrace to the nations in whose midst they occurred; defenseless Jews were robbed and ravished and shot down when they tried to protect themselves. Kuyper was opposed to anti-Semitism in any form, and he pointed to a solution to the Jewish problem—the establishment of a Jewish state, possibly even in the eastern part of Russia.

Kuyper's concluding words about the Jews took the form of a description of Palestine:

> A pious rabbi once compared the Holy Land to a human eye. Around that eye, the world. The white of that eye, Palestine. The apple of the eye, Zion, the image of God Himself. That imagery of Zion was realized in Christ: "He who has seen me has seen the Father." *That* is what happened in Palestine, and it is Palestine's abiding glory.

In *Antirevolutionaire Staatkunde* (Anti-Revolutionary Politics), his last major work, Kuyper again discussed anti-Semitism and stated that no such trend had manifested itself in The Netherlands. "The Calvinists appreciated the Old Testament more than the Lutherans did and therefore were impelled by a warm love for the ancient people and increasingly expected a revival of the Jewish people, also in the future."[14]

Some Jews felt hurt by what Kuyper had written and accused him of anti-Semitic feelings.[15] Indeed, his judgment was not always to the point, but on the whole I would underscore Dr. P. Kasteel's conclusion. After quoting Kuyper extensively on the subject, Kasteel wrote:

> It is impossible to deny that Kuyper knew the affairs of Israel and was interested in the Jewish problem. That knowledge and that interest have been matched by very few in The Netherlands. Only an irritated critic could call a man an anti-Semite after hearing him say: "The Jewish nation is and remains exceptional . . . The Jews are not a disappearing people; Israel remains."[16]

Back in Parliament

When Kuyper returned from his grand tour, he hesitated for a while before participating in active politics again. In 1907, on the occasion of his seventieth birthday, he was interviewed by a Roman Catholic journalist, who asked him whether he would be available for a vacant seat in the House of Commons. He replied that he was still busy finishing his book *Om de oude wereldzee* and that he was not as healthy as he would like to be; he stopped working at nine o'clock each evening, which he had not done earlier in his life. Apparently his energy did not flow as freely as it had earlier. Kuyper had to slow down.[17]

When he was elected to parliament in a by-election the next year, he accepted. From then on he again served as chairman of the Anti-Revolutionary faction in parliament. On the whole he supported the cabinet. His old influence was always apparent at the annual meeting of the delegates.

In 1909 he delivered his great speech "We Calvinists." That year was the four hundredth anniversary of Calvin's birth. In his oration Kuyper stressed both the fact of the *antithesis* and the necessity of *coalition*.

The antithesis had been present ever since the Lord had said He would "put enmity" (Genesis 3:15). It had revealed itself most forcefully, however, after the great revolution of 1789:

> Then a fundamental struggle began over the question whether the main political principles are to be derived from the *will of man* or from the *will of God*. Here you find the origin of the motto "Against the Revolution the Gospel." The antithesis is not the product of fantasy, nor has it been constructed by anyone. It *is* there. It *exists*, and it dominates our whole life.[18]

As for coalition, which meant political cooperation with the Roman Catholics, Kuyper stressed the necessity of joining forces with all who confessed the name of Jesus Christ. In earlier years he had been an anti-papist and had not agreed with the advice given by Groen van Prinsterer in his final years, namely, that in political matters the Calvinists should join forces as much as possible with their ancient sworn enemies. Later he recognized that circumstances had changed, and he became a friend of the great Roman Catholic politician Schaepman. He coined the phrase that the Protestant Christians of his time were still "rooted in the same soil of faith" as the Roman Catholics. In his last great political work he wrote:

> Our people became increasingly aware of the fact that the liberals and radicals had broken essentially with Christianity, which occasioned the assumption that there was still a Christian element present not only among the believing Protestants but also—if only partially—among the Roman Catholics. In ecclesiastical matters the sharp contrast was still there, but in social and political matters the old contrast was transformed into unanimous resistance against the modern, atheistic and materialistic view of life.[19]

The main work Kuyper wrote during this period of his life was *Pro Rege*, which I have already dealt with. Perhaps it could be called the climax of his efforts. It was followed by one of the most charming studies he ever wrote—a book dealing with the liturgy of the church.

Our Worship Services

There were at least three reasons why Kuyper, in 1897, began a series of articles on the liturgy of the church. He had to discontinue this labor of love in 1901, when he became prime minister. He finally brought this project to a conclusion in 1911, when he brought out these articles in the form of a book entitled *Onze eeredienst* (Our Worship Services).

His first reason for writing on this subject was historical. During his student years Kuyper had studied the life and work of a Lasco, the Polish reformer who, for some years, had been the superintendent of the congregation of Dutch refugees in London. While he was in his first parsonage, Kuyper published a Lasco's *Opera* (Works). A Lasco had provided that first Dutch Reformed church with a splendid liturgy,[20] leading Kuyper to declare in a later essay: "Our church would be liturgically less inferior if it had borrowed something from the London order of worship."[21]

His second reason for the book was pastoral. While he was still a minister of the established church, Kuyper had often protested against the arbitrariness of colleagues who changed the forms of worship on the basis of their own insights. A blantant example was the change made in the form of baptism. Now Kuyper was no formalist; he did not regard the forms of the church as sacrosanct, but could well envision changing them. However, he maintained that pastoral concern for the congregation required that such changes be not an expression of novelties discovered by some progressive pastor; rather, such changes could only be made by the common consent of the church at its major assemblies.

The third reason for his interest in liturgy was that Kuyper was a man of *good taste*. Despite the fact that he was often involved in fiery polemics, he appreciated good manners. In a speech which he had delivered in North America, he emphasized both warmth and dignity in the worship service:

> Certainty of faith, resting on the dogmas of election and the perseverance of the saints, has more than once been asserted in such a cold and outward way as to bring down the mystical union with Christ to the freezing point. Justification by faith alone has too often become an excuse for the uncharitable and lazy to abstain from, if not to jest at, Christian works. And in our holy services both the ear and the eye were, and still are, frequently offended.[22]

As Kuyper himself made plain, he had not intended to compose a scholarly treatise on liturgy. He preferred to adopt a conversational tone, so that his discussion would be of service not only to ministers but also to the membership at large.[23] He succeeded to such a remarkable degree that Dr. J.H. Gunning, Jr., a minister in the established church, expressed his thankfulness by hailing Kuyper as a "father in Christ."[24]

In an almost offhand manner, Kuyper discussed the manner and character of all the elements that make up a Reformed worship service. He gave a beautiful description of an altar: "The altar is a hand of God rising from the soil of the earth to receive the gift of man, namely, his sacrifice."[25] Reformed churches have no altars because the one sacrifice of Christ is sufficient forever. The Lord's table has taken the place of the altar; believers come to the Lord's table to receive the holy sacrament.

Yet, Kuyper said, we should not fall into the error of the spiritualism that does not appreciate any fixed forms. On the contrary, following in the footsteps of Calvin and a Lasco, we should treasure a sober, well ordered and meaningful liturgy.

Kuyper appreciated liturgical prayers but criticized some of the prayers prescribed for use in Reformed worship services on the grounds that they were too long-winded. He preferred some of the collects in the Anglican Book of Common Prayer.[26] He deplored the fact that many public prayers contained a great deal of reasoning and very little beseeching. Free Prayer is often a temptation to deliver a small sermon in the form of a prayer. In such cases a short formulary prayer is to be preferred.

Kuyper's criticism climbed to unusual heights when he wrote about preachers who seek human praise:

> In my view, that preacher is contemptible who, in his ministry of the Word, serves himself, and, after having preached, does not ask himself whether he has elevated souls to God and has comforted and blessed them but tries to find out everywhere whether his sermon was beautiful and whether it gripped the audience and exalted his name as a preacher. Preachers who act in such a manner should be deposed.[27]

Kuyper discussed the architecture of church buildings and pleads for a modern classroom in which to give catechism instruction—a room on a par with modern school facilities. He also discussed the meaning of the votum, which is followed by the benediction as the testimony of God's fatherly love toward His congregations. He pointed to the importance of the reading of the Ten Commandments each Sunday as a reminder of the will of God. On this point he differed with Calvin, for Kuyper wants the law to be read at the end of the worship service. He also declared himself in favor of kneeling during prayer in the worship service.

Kuyper's discussion of the public confession of sin and the absolution which follows it ends with this summary:

> The following is required in the worshp services: (1) a short admonition to remember our sins, (2) a common confession of guilt, preferably to be sung, and (3) a public announcement of forgiveness for those who have confessed sincerely, accompanied by an announcement of judgment for those who persevere in sin.
>
> This means a public action in three parts, not excluding the private, daily confession to God or the private confession to an intimate friend, when our conscience calls for it. It should be added, however, that this entire action in the public worship service requires the utmost devotion of the minister of

the Word. Every mechanical action judges itself, and a minister of the Word who does not personally confess along with his audience is unable to elicit the confession of others. What is required is calmness, clarity, and yet a toning down of the voice, and pauses between the parts of the action. No affectation or theatrics . . . being personally touched in the heart. This makes for community with God and Christ, our High Priest, who lives to pray for us.

But alas! How far we are still removed from this beauty in Zion.[28]

I would love to quote many other passages from this profound and practical book, but I must draw the line somewhere. I will conclude my treatment of it by quoting again from Dr. Gunning, who declared: "Dr. Kuyper appears in this book as a man of unbroken strength. He is still the same master in the vast field of the worship services as he was in the many other areas in which he made his powerful voice heard."

Friendship

In the first part of this chapter I pointed out that during this period of his life, Kuyper experienced growing opposition from certain quarters within his own party. Naturally, this situation sometimes depressed him. On the one hand he was almost idolized by his rank-and-file followers, but on the other hand he felt that, through the force of circumstances, he was being shifted gradually to the sidelines.

The question arises: Did Kuyper experience real friendship? Did he have personal friends? In response to this question, I must emphasize first of all that Kuyper's home was his castle. He often wrote about the value and blessing of good, well ordered family life,[29] and he certainly practiced what he preached.

In 1902, the year his wife died, Kuyper was visited by Mrs. C.A. Mason, an American author. In the March 3 issue of *De Standaard*, Mrs. Mason recorded her impressions of the home on the Prins Hendrikkade and informed her readers about the way she was received there. In the evening they all chatted together around the dinner table. All of Kuyper's sons and daughters were present, and Kuyper talked about his favorable impressions of American life, not neglecting to add that the leaders in America were totally mistaken in espousing the theory of evolution, for this theory was completely untenable.* Then Mrs. Mason continued:

> When dinner was over the housemaids entered and sat down; each one received a Bible. Dr. Kuyper selected a passage of Scripture and read it. Then all knelt down. He prayed with an admirable warmth and eloquence. We rose and had the feeling that the modern world was far away, and that its end was approaching.[30]

And we can rest assured that the events in the Kuyper home that evening were not arranged especially for Mrs. Mason's benefit. Dr. J. Van Lonkhuyzen, an American minister who had studied at the Free University, wrote in 1920:

> I have seen him and heard him, and nothing impressed me more than when Kuyper, in deep humility, bowed with his family before God. He could be high—he was one of the ten most important people—but he could also come down very low. I will never forget how he visited me, a young student, after an illness and disclosed his heart to me, as a friend speaking to a friend. He could repel people, but he could also attract them. He has made enemies, but with his winning ways he has also made friends who were very much attached to him, friends who, if need be, would go through fire and water for him.[31]

Kuyper was a friend to his students, a friend to his staff at the Free University,[32] and a friend to the workmen at the printing office of *De Standaard*. When the silver anniversary of the paper was celebrated in 1897, it was proposed that these workmen not be invited because the meeting hall would be rather crowded if they were there. Kuyper protested. He declared that when the night for the celebration came, he wanted to see all the typesetters and deliverymen and newsmen there, along with their wives; otherwise he would be very disappointed. Of course they were all there, and they presented their popular editor with an exquisite memorial medal. This fact is all the more impressive in view of the fact that most of these men were social democrats![33]

---

* Kuyper devoted extensive criticism to this theory in *Evolutie,* his rectoral oration of 1899.

Kuyper had some very special friends among the common Reformed people. I will mention only the names of J. Bechtold and H.I. Dibbetz, who were both members of the Amsterdam church when Kuyper arrived there. They had no special function and they certainly were not intellectuals, but they possessed a deep spiritual insight into Scripture and became Kuyper's personal friends. In the days of the Doleantie, when Kuyper had no time to spare, hardly a week went by without him taking time for an hourly visit with father Bechtold. He would listen like a child to what this brother told him about the ways of the Lord.[34] And when Dibbetz died in 1874, he wrote a tender letter of comfort to his widow, in which we find these words: "I am almost certain that he still thought of me in his last moments. So much were we one—one in heart and soul!"[35]

There were other dear friends who could be mentioned, such as Groen Van Prinsterer. Kuyper carried on an extensive correspondence with Groen until his death. L.W.F. Keuchenius, the short-term Anti-Revolutionary minister, was also one of Kuyper's bosom friends. Keuchenius died in 1893, and Kuyper devoted a short study to his life.* Above all, I should mention his faithful Achetes, F.L. Rutgers, co-leader of the Doleantie, who was Kuyper's colleague from the start at the Free University. For many years Kuyper drew on his incredible accuracy and his unfathomable knowledge of Calvin and Calvinism. When Rutgers died, Kuyper exclaimed: "I will miss no one as much as him."[36]

Not to be forgotten is the Amsterdam businessman Willem Hovy, who prayed and read the Bible with his workmen at the beginning of each day. Hovy was as much attached to the Moravian Brethren as to the principles of Calvinism. He was an undaunted supporter of Kuyper, and when he died Kuyper wrote: "For almost half a century I enjoyed his friendship."[37]

In the final period of his life, two outstanding men came very close to Kuyper's heart. One was A.W.F. Idenburg, a nobleman who had been colonial secretary in Kuyper's cabinet and later became governor-general of the Dutch East Indies. The other was H. Colijn, who was also a colonial expert and later

* *Mr. Levinus Wilhelminus Keuchenius* (1895). Kuyper named one of his children after Keuchenius. The book contains an unforgettable description of Keuchenius on his deathbed, where he miraculously regained his speech.

became prime minister. Both men trusted Kuyper without reservation, and Kuyper trusted them. Idenburg visited Kuyper daily at the sickbed that was to be his deathbed. Shortly before his death Kuyper asked Idenburg to assure all his many friends that "God was his refuge and his strength, a very present help in trouble."[38]

Character

The judgments that have been offered of Kuyper's character vary enormously. He has been called a very sincere Christian, but he has also been branded a very insincere actor. He has been praised for his eloquence, but he has likewise been condemned for his theatrics. He has been hailed as the "bellringer of the small people," but he has also been characterized as a demagogue. Kasteel, a Roman Catholic biographer who is quite sympathetic to Kuyper, speaks of him as "aggressive and intransigent, democratic but also dictatorial and aristocratic." Kasteel adds that Kuyper cut like a plow through hearts and brains.[39]

Many assessments have been offered, and anyone who takes the trouble to read the various memorial books written to commemorate key anniversaries in Kuyper's life and career will find many more than the ones I have mentioned here. (Memorial books were published in 1897, 1907, 1920, and 1937.) It is my own view that Kuyper provided a very important clue to the hidden depths of his own character when he described his conversion in *Confidentie,* the book I dealt with earlier. He tells us there how he broke down completely after reading a certain passage in *The Heir of Redclyffe.* Kuyper had identified with the anti-hero of the book, Philip Morville. He tells us that he admired this brilliant and successful young man, until he found out that the real hero of the story was Guy, his humble, self-denying cousin. The anti-hero breaks down at a certain moment, and it seems that Kuyper also broke down when he read that passage, for it was the eve of his conversion to God.

Kuyper had recognized himself—his own ambitions and his own weaknesses. By and large, Kuyper had the ability to do whatever he wanted: he could become a first-rate scholar, a mighty leader in all areas of life, or a man of the cultural elite. Kuyper was well aware that all these possibilities lay open before him. But once he read *The Heir of Redclyffe* he began his struggle for humility. He tried to become a servant of the often despised people of God. From then on, that struggle was to be central to his life.

And that struggle was often in conflict with a definite trend in his character. More than once it has been observed that Kuyper was something of a *caesar*.* He dominated people and situations with ease, and with his almost encyclopedic knowledge he could easily crush an opponent in a flood of logical arguments. It is an understandable and unmistakeable fact that this approach on Kuyper's part was not always accepted with good grace.

Others have commented on a second trait in his character: Kuyper has been called a *dreamer*.** For my part, I would prefer the term *visionary*. Kuyper had a great vision of the truly Reformed church that was yet to be. He had his vision of a nation that would bow before Jesus—*pro rege*. He tried to realize his vision by all the means at his disposal, and he once spoke of it in the following poetic terms:

> For me, one goal controls my being,
>   One high urge controls my soul,
> And I would rather die and perish
>   Ere I would lose that holy goal.
> 't Is to restore God's holy order,
>   In home and church, in school and state,
> In spite of all the world's resistance,
>   To all our nation's benefit.[40]

One goal! Kuyper dreamed his dream of a free church in a free state, and he tried to realize that vision by all available means.

He knew how to use those means, and this brings us to a third trait in his character: he was *a born strategist*. It was not by chance that his two closest friends during the last years of his life, Colijn and Idenburg, had both been professional soldiers. They knew respect and obedience, and they knew tactics.

---

* "In him was the nature of a caesar; he had dominating features; he was a kind of titan" (*De Beukelaar*, Nov. 19, 1920).
** G. Puchinger has written: "He was the great master dreamer of the nineteenth century" (*Gesprek over de onbekende Kuyper*, published in 1971).

Kuyper himself had soldier's blood in his veins. One of his grandfathers had been an officer in the Swiss Guard. Thus it should not surprise us that he liked to use military terminology. In 1897 he looked back and observed:

> When I arrived in Utrecht, I imagined I would find in that fortress, that Jerusalem of The Netherlands, some very learned brethren defending the fortress with the weapon of the Word—not just standing on the walls but even sallying forth from the gates to attack the enemy. What did I find? . . . only some weak defenses, soldiers waiting for the first shot to be fired by the other side . . . officers and troops that did not trust each other . . . a totally defective plan of defense. I felt that this was a totally wrong attitude for a battalion that called itself the army of the living God.[41]

As a competent general, Kuyper organized his army. He organized the opposition to the liberal synod when he was a minister or an elder in Utrecht and Amsterdam. He organized the opposition to the monopoly position held by the public school. He organized the Anti-Revolutionary Party, overlooking no details in the process.

Closely connected with Kuyper's emphasis on a comprehensive strategy was his insistence on *clear-cut positions*. He wanted to call a spade a spade. When he learned from Groen van Prinsterer that the public school was no longer a Christian school, he wanted to say so openly. When the ethical theologians tried to walk the tightrope between orthodoxy and modern theology, he exposed their ambiguities.

Nor could he refrain from criticism when Herman Bavinck, then a young professor at Kampen, gave a speech in 1884 in which he said of the ethical theology that "there were some elements in it that kept him from expressing his complete agreement with it." Kuyper, who regarded Bavinck highly, called this value judgment an overdose of courtesy and asked:

> Is that allowed? When you have first concluded that someone's theology is in conflict with Scripture, that it contains more philosophy than Christian truth, that it suffers from pantheism, that it obscures the borderline between the Creator and the creature to a certain extent—are you then allowed to declare of such a thoroughly dangerous theology, which for decades has seduced the best among us, that you do not completely agree with it?[42]

Kuyper would loathe the contemporary dialogue situation that grants everyone his say without ever arriving at the truth. Yet I should hasten to add that he was *not a dogmatist* who recognized only one type of Christian or one type of church. It has even been said that he was as much a man of synthesis as of antithesis,[43] for he often saw that there were two sides to a question. Indeed, even though he criticized the ethical theologians severely, he considered prominent representatives of the theology as his brothers. At first he was an "anti-papist" and he always stressed the irreconcilable contrast between the Reformation and Rome, but he considered Schaepman, the great Roman Catholic statesman, a fellow believer and promoted a "coalition" with the Roman Catholics as his allies against modernism.

More than once Kuyper cautioned against being too rash or too dogmatic in one's judgment. It must have surprised many people that after offering an eloquent plea for discipline in the church, he interrupted himself by writing:

> It should never offend you that not everyone follows your exact example. There are no fixed rules here that can be maintained with great precision in all possible situations. The situations differ widely, and the results of the situation often differ even more widely. Let us not judge each other, but rather allow our King to be Judge of each one's conscience.[44]

He was fully aware of the power of historical conditions, and elsewhere he wrote: "Rash reformers always spoil the future. Only he who proceeds with caution may hope to improve future conditions."[45]

At bottom Kuyper was a man with a *tender heart*. It is touching to read about the tears in his eyes when the students at the Free University offered him a token of their appreciation,[46] although by that time he was an old man. But what tenderness of heart we find in his last letter to the dying Groen Van Prinsterer, and in his letter of comfort to Mrs. Dibbetz, and in all his meditations!

He was often impatient, and sometimes unfair. Yet it was all bound up with his love for Christ and his desire for the coming of His Kingdom. It was on the basis of his own experience that Kuyper wrote:

> Patience is one of the holy adornments with which Jesus Himself adorns the soul after He has cleansed it with His

righteousness. Patience is a fruit of the Spirit. Its seed is not within us. Its branches twine around the cross of Christ; its goal is in eternity; its glory is in the grace of God. Patience ought to be the possession of every child of God. If it is not his when he is reborn, it ought to grow within him as he grows in Christ. But it is sadly lacking among us. This is evident from our restlessness, from our aversion to the cross, even though we hide that aversion behind a veil of resignation . . . We need patience . . . to revive the song of praise as we bear the cross which His love assigns to us.[47]

Chapter 16

Finishing Touches

Summing Up

In 1917, when he had reached the age of the very strong, the second volume of Kuyper's last magnum opus appeared—*Antirevolutionaire Staatkunde* (Anti-Revolutionary Politics). The first volume was 728 pages in length, the second 654. It was indeed an impressive achievement. Kuyper had worked on this project in his customary manner, following a regular, steady pace.

In 1915 he had discussed the project with his publisher, J.H. Kok of Kampen. He had not yet written a word, and he still needed some time to complete the preliminary study, for there were a few more books he had to read before he began to write. "When do you think you will be finished?" the publisher asked. "I'll tell you in just a moment, Mr. Kok," Kuyper replied. He took a pencil in hand and began to calculate. "So much on Monday, on Tuesday only an hour, so much on Wednesday, nothing on Thursday . . . In total that adds up to so many hours per week. In an hour I can write . . . thus . . ." After some more figuring Kuyper concluded: "If nothing stands in the way I can hand in the last copy in December of 1916. You can count on it."[1]

Kuyper's timing proved accurate. He tells us in his introduction that increasing deafness caused him to spend most of his time in his study, which had enabled him to fulfill a long-time desire of his heart, namely, to write a better-organized and more comprehensive textbook for the members of the Anti-Revolutionary Party than *Ons Program,* which he had written many years before. He certainly succeeded in writing a readable and substantial work, containing many historical reminiscences. Many themes touched on earlier in Kuyper's writings reappear. In a sense the book represented a summing up of his political convictions.

Kuyper was still the old warrior. As he wrote about the rupture in the party in 1894, which arose from his conflict with Lohman, he stated that it was unavoidable because it had a social background. He then continued: "It is an undeniable fact that the capitalistic and aristocratic powers in our country hauled down the banner of the cross, and that, after the terrible apostasy of the last part of the nineteenth century, only in the countryside, among the lower middle classes and the workmen, were there people who kept going the way of their fathers."[2] Yet it is evident that Kuyper had mellowed. Listen to the following apology:

> I have been blamed—not only by the opposition—for holding the reins too tight, both in the Anti-Revolutionary Party and at the annual meetings of its delegates. I don't want to deny that this reproach has some validity, but I do want to add that it was the totally natural result of three circumstances: (1) that I was the one who started the organization, (2) that I was the editor of the leading paper for about half a century, and (3) that since 1872 I was always charged with the task of leading the annual meeting of the delegates, which is a difficult job. I don't want to deny that I sometimes make mistakes, and I concede that this must have irritated other excellent leaders of the party at times; yet I would ask anyone who criticizes me for these reasons to take into account the great difficulties of my task. I plead extenuating circumstances, without trying to present myself as one who is innocent as a lamb.[3]

Important and of current interest is Kuyper's insistence on the historical reliability of the first eleven chapters of the book of Genesis. As he writes about the origins of law and justice, he rejects and refutes the theory of evolution in unmistakable terms, emphasizing that it was God Himself who revealed the original structure of the world.*

---

* "The animal world is not a product of Evolution, but it was created by God Almighty in one moment, with its total structure and with its inner organism. It is evident, therefore, that the same almighty power of God must have been able to change it all in one moment, so that the once peaceful organization changed into a destructive one" (*Antirevolutionaire Staatkunde,* I, p. 51). "He revealed fundamental law-principles in the first nine chapters of Genesis, namely, what He Himself expressed in words" (p. 79; see also p. 84).

Also of current interest is what Kuyper wrote about abortion and pacifism. Concerning the former, he quotes with approval a speech given by Kouwer, an Utrecht professor, who had expressed indignation at the fact that 80,000 abortions ("crimes against the human seed") were perpetrated annually in New York. He also pointed to the position taken by Pope Pius IX, who had declared that the embryo should be acknowledged to be a human being from the moment of conception.

When we consider the question of pacifism, we should bear in mind that Kuyper wrote this book during the first world war. In the first volume he expresses some understanding—and also sympathy—when he looks at pacifism.[4] At the same time he hints at the utopian character of this dream.[5] In the second volume he devotes a chapter, which bristles with expertise, to how the fatherland is to be defended. In this chapter he stresses that there are conditions which any just war must meet,[6] but he remains silent about the problem of pacifism. The conditions for a just war are that the independence or integrity of the kingdom must be at stake, and that all other means to resolve the issue must first be tried.

Also important is what Kuyper writes about the government that rules by the grace of God but is nevertheless *not* a theocracy. The situation in Israel was unique and is not to be repeated. Society is not created by the state; it possesses its own God-given sovereignty. Here Kuyper speaks of the family, the church, science, art, technology, discoveries, trade, industry, agriculture, hunting and fishing, and free social organizations.[7]

It is clear that we do not find a scientific arrangement or analysis or system here. Kuyper looked at the fullness of life as it had developed in his own time. He was not in favor of a dictatorial state but hoped that the government would recognize the special character of all those spheres of life, would support them when they asked for support, and would intervene with its legislative power only when the spheres were in danger of colliding.

It should be added that although Kuyper grouped the church among the corporations that enjoy a sovereignty of their own, he also emphasized the church's unique character. The church is not an association among other associations, for it was founded not by man but by Christ the King. It is the beginning of the eternal kingdom which will encompass heaven and earth. Kuyper believed that his ideal of a free church in a free state had been most fully realized in the United States of America.[8]

As for the social problem, Kuyper maintained that it is the government's responsibility to develop up-to-date social legislation, but the main impulse and the necessary arrangements should be initiated by the laborers themselves. The government should make up a complete list of employers and employees, in order to unite them in a union (each group on its own, but with contact between the two groups). This body should then advise the government so that solutions can be found for the problems that occur. Fundamental differences (e.g. between Christians, socialists and Roman Catholics) can entail special organizations. As long as the ideal is not attained, arbitration is the solution.*

I have given only a few samples of the contents of this work in which we find so many of the themes and phrases Kuyper had developed over the years. The book was a summing up, and executed in such a respectable and entertaining way that we don't know which to admire more, the old man's indomitable energy or the sincere confession of faith that shines through on all the pages.

Sub Specie

In earlier years Kuyper had expressed the hope of finishing his career by writing a commentary on one of the books of the Bible. When *Van de voleinding (On the Consummation,* i.e. of all things) was published, he did not quite realize that desire, but he did come close. Some years later part of this lengthy work was translated into English and published under the title *The Revelation of St. John.*

In his later years much more than in his earlier years, Kuyper was preoccupied with the question of the signs that would precede the second coming of Christ. He had already

---

* *Antirevolutionaire Staatkunde*, II, pp. 534, 544. W. Speelman's comment that Kuyper, by transferring the social problem to the area of politics, had abandoned the sovereignty of the sphere of labor is not well founded (see *In Rapport met de Tijd*, 1980, p. 178).

spoken about those signs in 1871, when he issued an impressive appeal for repentance.[9] In 1912 he declared that the missionary activities of the church should be multiplied, for the second coming of Christ would be preceded by the Christianization of the nations. He added that there were many more things that would announce His coming again.[10] In a casual speech to young people in 1915 Kuyper pointed to the terrors of the first world war as a fulfillment of one of the Savior's prophetic signs. He warned against a false orthodoxy that confesses with its lips that Christ will come back one day but never seriously considers the possibility that he will come back *now*, in our own lifetime. Kuyper ended this speech with an exhortation to the young people to pray from the heart: "Come, Lord Jesus, yes, come soon."[11]

Now Kuyper finally tackled in a systematic manner the questions concerning the final end of the history of the church and the world. The fruits of his labors appeared as a series of articles in *De Heraut*, his weekly paper, from 1911 to 1918. The articles contained not just a commentary on the last book of the Bible but also an exposition of the expectation of the great kingdom that is to come, that hope which we find running through all of Scripture.

Kuyper would not have been Kuyper if he had not started by discussing the universal idea of a coming situation of bliss and if he had not discussed such utopian prospects as we find them in various philosophical systems. But neither would he have been the man he was if he had not taken his definite point of departure, under the tutelage of Scripture, in the eternal counsel of God, which guarantees that nothing happens by chance and guarantees that God must one day be everything to everyone.

The consummation of God's decree does not just affect man in soul and body; the divine decree affects heaven and earth, man and angel, animal and plant—the total creation of God. Kuyper described how God's grace had wrestled throughout history against the consequences of sin, and how the ascension of Christ was the great turning-point in that history. Only in the last part of this substantial work did he offer an exposition of the book of Revelation; this was the part that has been translated into English.

The value of this book does not match Kuyper's earlier theological works. He was in his eighties by the time he wrote the last part. It was prepared for publication in book form by his son, Dr. H.H. Kuyper, who introduced certain revisions and admitted that the book contained a certain amount of repetition and also strayed from the subject here and there. Even so, the book has a grandeur of its own. "As we read it, we are transported into a great cathedral for a little while. We are impressed by our own smallness."[12] And we can well understand why its author wrote at the very end: "It behooves us quietly to thank and adore God, who granted us the privilege of completing this study at our advanced age" (December 15, 1918).

Death

The year 1918 was marked by revolutionary turmoil in The Netherlands. At the end of the great war it seemed for a while as though the fire of the German revolution would spread to The Netherlands. Then the queen would be deposed, and The Netherlands would become a republic with the socialist leader Peter Jelles Troelstra as its president.

Troelstra was a Frisian, but the majority of the Frisians did not agree with him.* From November 14 through November 16, thousands of demobilized soldiers arrived at the royal residence in The Hague in order to protect their queen. Among the soldiers were many Frisians, and among the Frisians were many supporters of Kuyper. On the evening of March 18 they marched to Canal Street, where the old leader lived. They sang several national hymns and finally the words of the familiar psalm: "Jehovah bless thee from above."

Kuyper was visibly moved, and he addressed them: "My time has passed; in your hands lies the future . . . Your coming here is a sign from my God that after He has called me from this life the principles which are precious to me above all else will live on in the younger generation—also in you." Then he asked them to sing two of his favorite psalms: "How blessed, Lord, are they

---

* Friesland, one of the northern provinces of The Netherlands, still boasts its own language. The character of the Frisians is marked by independence of judgment.

who know the joyful sound" and "Thou art, O God, our boast, the glory of our power; Thy sovereign grace is e'er our fortress and our tower."[13] It was one of the last great moments of his life.

His strength declined, and by the time he celebrated his eighty-third birthday (October 29, 1920) he was very ill. He died not long afterward, on the 8th of November. His close friend Idenburg then wrote the following words in *De Standaard:*

> I had the privilege of visiting him during the last months, and I saw him almost daily during the last weeks. I have witnessed moments when he suffered bodily, but never was his faith assaulted. I found him always resting in his God, even when his body was (if only briefly) in unrest. For weeks he expected the time of his departure, which he desired ardently. To be with Christ was by far the best to him. What this long time of lying quietly in bed meant for him can be understood only by those who knew his restless urge to work, which was with him right to the last moment. His faith always remained clear. His sickbed led to a strengthening of the faith of all who nursed him.
>
> More than once I talked with him about the faithful love of a large group of his fellow believers—"our people," as he used to say. I thanked him for all that he, by the grace of God, had meant to them.
>
> A short time ago, when he saw that the end was approaching, he demanded that I tell them that God was his refuge and his strength and a very present help in trouble.
>
> And so he went from us, just as he lived among us, glorying in the power and grace of his God.[14]

He was carried to his grave on the 12th of November. Following his instructions, the inscription on his tomb was:

Dr. A. Kuyper
Born October 29, 1837
And fallen asleep in his Savior
November 8, 1920

Influence

Kuyper was a giant who straddled the nineteenth and twentieth centuries. His life bridged the closing of one era and the opening of another. By his influence, conservatism was conquered, liberalism thwarted and socialism checked. Reformed theology was renewed, honesty in the church was proclaimed, the confession was honored, and the kingship of Christ was professed.

In the area of politics, it should be noted that many of Kuyper's fellow believers were either stalwart conservatives or emotional children of the Dutch Réveil when he appeared on the scene. The conservatives believed in the Christian character of the nation; they were proud to be Dutch and did not want to change the prevailing situation. The men of the Réveil represented a Dutch branch of Methodism; they were zealous for the winning of souls and committed to all manner of philanthropy, but shy of anything that looked like concentrated Christian political or social action.

When Groen van Prinsterer, who was himself a son of the Réveil, broke radically with all conservatism in 1874, Kuyper was one of the men he chose to do what Groen himself had always hoped to accomplish, namely, lead the nation, in all areas of its life, back to the confession of its fathers. Yet there was a marked difference between Groen and Kuyper. Groen had many excellent qualities, but he was neither an organizer nor a legislator. Thorbecke, the great champion of liberalism, once said to him in parliament: "The esteemed speaker struggles incessantly, but he leaves not the slightest trace of what he wants or aims at in any law."[15] It was not without reason, then, that Dr. L.W.G. Scholten once made the following comparison:

> Groen was the general without an army who took it for granted that his ideas would be put to practical use by others. Kuyper created a well-organized party, cooperating with allies on an equal basis; he was in a hurry to do himself and to reap himself what his ideas called for as the need of the hour.
>
> Groen always refused to mold the political reforms he desired into the form of an elaborate system. He always trusted the persons of his coworkers and was always tragically disappointed in their deeds. Kuyper, with his powerful grasp, forged a massive political system and in this way burdened his successors with finding the congruence between the actual situation and the system.[16]

Kuyper completed what Groen had begun and dared to be radical in drawing the practical consequences. Groen had promoted an increasing democracy, but at heart he was an aristocrat. Kuyper was a complete democrat—although not in the vulgar sense of the word. As we have seen, he was the man of the "small people." He knew the ins and outs of their daily life. He was aware of what went on in the smallest towns and villages in The Netherlands.

What Kuyper stood for was qualified democracy. The source of all authority lay never in the people but in God alone. What Kuyper strove for was not to see people ruling over people but a recognition of the organic composition of all areas of life. Thus he pleaded for the extension of the right to vote not to all the individuals in a nation but to all the heads of families. He pleaded for the independence (under God) of the various spheres of life, which were not created by the state and therefore should not be regulated by the government but should follow their own God-given calling, to be corrected by the state only in cases of overlap or conflict.

Groen had struggled all his life (after his conversion) for honesty in the church. He was the inspiring fighter who sought to uphold the basic principles of the classic Christian faith over against the Groningen school, the Moderns, and also—although with some hesitation—the Ethical theologians. Kuyper, after his arrival in Utrecht, called out with a loud voice for that same honesty. He was not afraid to take drastic measures and, in fact, loathed half-measures. He could find no rest before the church became truly Reformed, even though this led to a heart-breaking rupture. And he continued to express his desire for ongoing reformation.

It was a weakness of Groen's that, despite his laudable personal philanthrophic initiatives, he never offered a timely social program. Kuyper was the man of Christian social appeal. In this way, too, he was the right man at the right time.

He was as much opposed to the non-interference, *laissez-faire* policy of the liberals as to the socialists' idea of a state-controlled society. He wanted free laborers and free employers who would not carry on an endless and hopeless class-struggle but would instead look one another straight in the eye and arrange their contracts in an honorable manner. Any remaining differences would have to be settled by arbitration and be ratified by government legislation.

Kuyper was himself a free man. He was never a servant of men, and he was not afraid to speak the truth as he saw it, even if this meant that he would be estranged from people who had been his friends. He did not bow his knee to the baals of his time, whether in the form of scientism, mammonism, evolutionism, or culturism. He fought for a free church, a free Christian school, a free university, a free Christian labor movement, and a free Christian political party.

He wanted to be free—but always to remain bound by the infallible Word of God. He wanted to be free, but he always honored the believer's communion with the church of all ages, which comes to expression in the church's confessions.

Kuyper could be very tolerant, and he never forced any development into a revolutionary situation. He respected the laws of history, recognized different Christian communities, and acknowledged a pluriformity of churches. Yet he always drew the line when he sensed that people were not being true to their sacred commitments. In 1914 he wrote to the Board of the Free University: "If your association should decide to accept a doctor, that is, a teacher, an instructor, who would definitely deviate from the confession, rest assured that in such a case I would cut off every connection and contact with the Free University, and I would do so publicly."[17]

When Kuyper appeared on the scene, the Dutch nation, in its leadership and majority, had lost contact with its glorious past. Some liberals tried to revive that past by pointing to the great cultural achievements of the "golden age."[18] Kuyper emphasized the Calvinistic character of the nation and appealed to the energy, fearlessness and faith of the Reformation era.

When he died, free Christian schools were to be found from north to south. Believers were applying Christian principles in their homes, churches and associations. Christian men of science were demonstrating that belief in the Bible was not antiquated but up-to-date. The face of the country had been renewed.

Notes

Chapter 1

1. See O. Chadwick, *The Secularization of the European Mind in the Nineteenth Century* (1975), p. 11.
2. A. Kuyper, *Het Modernisme* (1871); *De Gemeene Gratie*, II (1905), pp. 27, 408-411.
3. E. Gewin, "Juliana von Krudener," in *Pietistische Portretten* (1922), pp. 50-53.
4. A. Kuyper, *Ons Program* (1880 edition), pp. 402, 403.
5. See H.G. Schenk, *De geest van de Romantiek* (1966), p. 13.
6. See E. Troeltsch, *Der Historismus und seine Probleme* (1922).
7. See M.C. d'Arcy, *The Meaning and Matter of History* (1959), p. 9.
8. *Kuyper-Gedenkboek 1897*, p. 72.
9. K. Scott Latourette, *A History of Christianity* (1953), p. 1193.
10. Quoted by P.A. Diepenhorst in his postscript to Groen's *Ongeloof en revolutie* (1922), pp. 270-271.
11. J. Dillenberger and C. Welch, *Protestant Christianity, Interpreted Through Its Development* (1954), p. 205.
12. The first words of his oration *Evolutie* (1899).
13. *Institutes,* I.3.1.
14. See A. C. McGiffert, *Protestant Thought Before Kant* (1961), p. 247.

Chapter 2

1. K. Barth, *Die Protestantische Theologie im 19. Jahrhundert* (1947), pp. 425-432.
2. K. Aner, *Kirchengeschichte*, Vol. IV (1931), p. 158.
3. Aner, p. 155.
4. *Verspreide geschriften* (1860), p. 16.
5. A. Kuyper, "Alexander Comrie," in *The Catholic Presbyterian* (1882).
6. A. Steenbeek, *Herman Munthinge* (1931).

7. J.C. Rullmann, in *Christelijke Encyclopaedie*, first edition, Vol. IV, p. 441.

8. P. Kasteel, *Abraham Kuyper* (1938), p. 44.

9. K. Barth, *Die Protestantische Theologie*, pp. 379-380.

10. A. Kuyper, *De Vleeschwording des Woords* (1887), p. 60.

11. A. Kuyper, *Encyclopaedie der heilige Godgeleerdheid*, Vol. I (1908²), p. 351.

12. B.M.G. Reardon, *Religious Thought in the Nineteenth Century* (1966), p. 44.

13. K. Barth, *Die Protestantische Theologie*, p. 400.

14. Barth, p. 377.

15. H. Bavinck, *Gereformeerde Dogmatiek*, Vol. I (1918), p. 140.

16. Dillenberger and Welch, *Protestant Christianity*, p. 189.

17. Schaff-Herzog's *Religious Encyclopedia*, Vol. III (1958 edition), p. 156.

18. A. Kuyper, *Eenige kameradviezen uit de jaren 1874 en 1875*, p. 196; see also *Ons Program*, pp. 148, 413.

Chapter 3

1. See A. Goslinga, *Willem I als verlicht despoot* (1918).

2. A. Kuyper, *De Leidse Professoren en de Executeurs der Dordtsche Nalatenschap* (1879), p. 83.

3. A. Kuyper, *Confidentie* (1873), p. 64.

4. J. Lindeboom, *Geschiedenis van het Vrijzinnig Protestantisme*, Vol. II (1930), p. 54.

5. G.J. Vos, *Groen van Prinsterer en zijn tijd*, Vol. I (1886), p. 81.

6. R.H. Bremmer, *Herman Bavinck als dogmaticus* (1961), p. 67.

7. P.A. van Leeuwen, *Het kerkbegrip in de theologie van Abraham Kuyper* (1946), p. 29.

8. H. Bavinck, *De Theologie van D. Chantepie de la Saussaye* (1884), pp. 84-86.

9. L. Knappert, *Geschiedenis van de Nederlands Hervormde Kerk gedurende de 18e en 19e eeuw* (1912), pp. 326, 327.

10. *Institutes*, I.7.

11. Belgic Confession, Article 5.

12. J.H. Scholten, *De Leer der Nederlands Hervormde Kerk*, Vol. I⁴ (1861), pp. 194-221.

13. K.H. Roessingh, *Het Modernisme in Nederland* (1922), p. 91.

14. Roessingh, p. 83.

Chapter 4

1. A. Kuyper, *Calvinism* (1961 edition), pp. 35, 36.

2. Several charming anecdotes about his childhood are to be

found in J.C. Rullmann, *Abraham Kuyper* (1928), Chapter 2.

3. See my book *Abraham Kuyper als kerkhistoricus* (1945), p. 17.
4. A. Kuyper, *Het Modernisme* (1871), p. 67.   *
5. *Confidentie*, p. 35.
6. *Confidentie*, p. 39.
7. Under the title *Disquisitio historico-theologica exhibens Johannis Calvini et Johannes a Lasco de Ecclesia sententiarum inter se compositionem.*
8. See my book *Abraham Kuyper als kerkhistoricus*, pp. 34ff.
9. *Confidentie*, p. 42.
10. *Confidentie*, p. 43.

Chapter 5

1. *Predicatiën* (1913), p. 5.
2. *Predicatiën*, p. 243.
3. *Predicatiën*, pp. 245-246.
4. A letter of January 28, 1865, in the Kuyper archive.
5. *Predicatiën*, p. 246.
6. *Confidentie*, p. 45.
7. See Article 22 of the Dort Church Order.

Chapter 6

1. J.C. Rullmann, *De strijd voor kerkherstel* (1928[3]), p. 160.
2. See S. Kierkegaard, *Attack upon "Christendom,"* trans. W. Lowrie (1959).
3. *Kuyper-Gedenkboek* (1897), p. 71.
4. T. de Vries, *G. Groen van Prinsterer in zijn omgeving* (1908), p. 115.
5. *Nederlandsche Gedachten*, August 19, 1871.
6. *Het beroep op het volksgeweten* (1869), pp. 17-18.
7. Rullmann biography, p. 50.
8. *Predicatiën*, pp. 327ff.
9. Rullmann biography, p. 54. Kuyper was to write extensively on this problem in *Uit het Woord*, Vol. I (1884).
10. *Kuyper-Gedenkboek* (1937), p. 216 (article by T. Ferwerda).
11. Rullmann biography, p. 55.
12. Rullmann, *De strijd voor kerkherstel*, p. 175.

Chapter 7

1. *De Standaard*, July 23, 1878.
2. *Souvereiniteit in eigen kring* (1880).
3. *The Herald*, October 3, 1880.

4. It was translated into English in 1904 and published in the *Bibliotheca Sacra*.

5. *Present-day Biblical Criticism in its Precarious Tendency for the Congregation of the Living God*, in *Bibliotheca Sacra* (1904), p. 414.

6. *Present-day Biblical Criticism*, p. 674.

7. *Present-day Biblical Criticism*, p. 684.

8. *Synopsis Purioris Theologiae* (1632 edition), p. 24.

9. *The Christian College in the Twentieth Century*, pp. 72ff.

10. *The Christian College*, p. 83.

11. On the Lohman affair, see P. Kasteel, *Abraham Kuyper*, pp. 195-202 and 327-333, and L.C. Suttorp, *A.F. De Savornin Lohman*, Chapters 5 and 10.

12. Letter to Lohman, February 10, 1890 (see Kasteel, p. 157).

13. *De Leidsche Professoren en de executeurs der Dordtsche nalatenschap* (1879), p. 83.

Chapter 9

1. *Het Conflict Gekomen*, II (1886), p. 41.

2. *Het Modernisme* (1871), p. 45.

3. *Laatste Woord* (1886), p. 7.

4. *Tractaat van de Reformatie der Kerken* (1883), p. 143.

5. *Tractaat*, pp. 112-115.

6. *Het Conflict Gekomen*, III (1886), p. 36.

7. J.C. Rullmann, *De Doleantie* (1917), p. 342.

8. V. Hepp, *Dr. Herman Bavinck* (1921), p. 180.

9. *The Implications of Public Confession*, trans. Henry Zylstra (1934), p. 49.

10. Hepp, *Dr. Herman Bavinck*, p. 182.

11. G. Puchinger and N. Scheps, *Gesprek over de onbekende Kuyper* (1971), p. 50.

12. T.F. Bensdorp, *Pluriformiteit* (1901), p. 10.

13. Article on Alexander Comrie in *The Catholic Presbyterian* (1882), p. 281.

14. See *E. Voto Dordraceno*, I, pp. 344ff; *Pro Rege*, II, p. 197; III, pp. 336ff.

15. *E. Voto Dordraceno*, II, p. 490.

16. *Verklaring van de Kerkordening van de Nationale Synode van Dordrecht van 1618-1619*, ed. J. de Jong (1918), p. 171.

17. For more details, see my book *Abraham Kuyper als kerkhistoricus* (1945), pp. 129ff.

Chapter 10

1. Baron B.J.L. de Geer to Kuyper on September 6, 1891 (see P. Kasteel, *Abraham Kuyper*, p. 203).

2. *Proces Verbaal Sociaal Congress 1891*, p. 106.
3. *Het sociale vraagstuk en de christelijke religie*, p. 40.
4. *Het sociale vraagstuk*, p. 71.
5. C.J. Mulder, *Het sociale leven en streven in verleden en heden*, Vol. II (no date), pp. 185ff.
6. *De Standaard*, February 3, 1903.
7. Kuyper, *Parliamentaire redevoeringen*, Vol. II, p. 334.
8. P. Kasteel, *Abraham Kuyper*, p. 271.
9. *Wat nu?* p. 21.

Chapter 11

1. T. Ferwerda, "Dr. Kuyper als hoogleraar," in *Gedenkboek 1937*, pp. 211ff.
2. In the United States by L. J. Hulst in *Supra en Infra*, and in The Netherlands by C. Veenhof in *Rondom 1905*.
3. See Canons of Dort, I, 7.
4. *E Voto Dordraceno*, II, pp. 170-172.
5. A.G. Honig, *Alexander Comrie* (1892), Introduction.
6. A. Kuyper, Jr., *Johannes Maccovius* (1899), Introduction.
7. Printed in Rullmann's *Bibliographie*, II, pp. 263ff.
8. *Institutes*, I.VI.2.
9. *Encyclopaedie der Heilige Godgeleerdheid*, II (1894); see also *De Gemene Gratie in Wetenschap en Kunst* (1905).
10. *Het Calvinisme*, pp. 125, 126.
11. *Bedoeld noch gezegd* (1885), p. 46.
12. *De Heraut,* December 7, 1877.
13. "Recent Dogmatic Thought in The Netherlands," in *The Presbyterian and Reformed Review* (April 10, 1892), p. 226.
14. See R.H. Bremmer, *Herman Bavinck als Dogmaticus* (1961), pp. 13-64.
15. Ernst Troeltsch called it a "Hineindeutung in den primitiven Genfer Calvinismus" (*Soziallehren*, 1923 edition, p. 607).
16. E. Troeltsch, *The Social Teachings of the Christian Churches*, II, 1960 edition, p. 688.
17. See my book *Abraham Kuyper als kerkhistoricus* (1945), pp. 138ff.
18. Especially in his *Publiek vermaak* (1881), which was co-authored by F.L. Rutgers; also in the second of his Stone Lectures (see *Calvinism*, published in 1899).
19. See my book *The Church in the Twentieth Century*, pp. 25ff.
20. See H. Beets, *The Christian Reformed Church* (1946), pp. 91, 92.
21. These conclusions were adopted by the synod of the Christian Reformed Church in 1908 (see L. Berkhof, *Systematic Theology*, 1972 edition, pp. 639-640).
22. T. Ferwerda, in *Gedenkboek 1937*, p. 221.

Chapter 12

1. *Predikatiën* (1913), p. 399.
2. *Ons Program* (1879), p. 30.
3. *Tractaat van de Reformatie der Kerken* (1883), p. 67.
4. See also *Confidentie* (1873), p. 5; *Calvinisme en Revisie* (1891), pp. 47-48; *Evolutie* (1899), p. 9.
5. *Briefwisseling van Mr. G. Groen van Prinsterer met Dr. A. Kuyper*, bewerkt door Dr. A. Goslinga (1937), pp. 58, 59, 67, 68, 217, 218.
6. E. Burke, *Speech on Reconciliation with America*, ed. Muller-Lage (1923), pp. 22, 24, 25.
7. Translated by J.H. De Vries (Oberlin, Ohio).
8. Rullmann, *Bibliographie*, III, p. 163.
9. Rullman, pp. 84-85.
10. *De positie van Nederland* (1917), p. 9.
11. *Varia Americana* (1889), pp. 7-8.
12. *Varia Americana*, p. 35.
13. *Varia Americana*, pp. 19, 144-151.
14. *Varia Americana*, p. 64.
15. *Varia Americana*, p. 81.
16. In an article by A.G. Mackay.
17. *Varia Americana*, p. 83.
18. *Calvinism,* pp. 28-29.
19. *Varia Americana*, pp. 131-132.
20. *Varia Americana*, pp. 50, 51.
21. *Varia Americana*, p. 133.
22. *Varia Americana*, p. 152.
23. *Varia Americana*, p. 168.
24. In the original Dutch it was called "Het Calvinisme in de Historie."
25. *Das Wesen des Christentums* (1900—English translation published in 1901).
26. *Calvinism*, p. 34.
27. *Calvinism*, pp. 22-23.
28. *Calvinism*, p. 14.
29. *Calvinism*, p. 34.
30. *Calvinism*, p. 33.
31. A.A. van Ruler, *Kuypers idee ener Christelijke cultuur* (1938).
32. S.J. Ridderbos, *De theologische cultuurbeschouwing van Abraham Kuyper* (1947), p. 286.
33. Ridderbos, p. 321.
34. *Anti-Revolutionaire Staatkunde*, I (1916), p. 627.

Chapter 13

1. Prof. T.L. Haitjema in *Op den uitkijk*, December 6, 1924.
2. *De navolging van Christus en het moderne leven* (1918), p. 32.
3. *Uit het Woord*, II (1875), p. 129.
4. J.H. Scholten, *De leer der Hervormde Kerk*, II (1862), pp. 26ff.
5. *Uit het Woord*, II, pp. 193-4.
6. *Uit het Woord* (Second Series: *Dat de genade particulier is*, 1879), pp. 250-251.
7. *Predicatiën* (1913), pp. 111ff.
8. *E Voto Dordraceno*, II, p. 192.
9. *E Voto Dordraceno*, II, p. 159.
10. *E Voto Dordraceno*, II, pp. 166-167.
11. *Uit het Woord* (1879), pp. 17-38.
12. *Uit het Woord* (1879), pp. 151ff.
13. *Uit het Woord* (1879), pp. 254-255.
14. *De algemeene genade,* p. 6.
15. See H. Kuiper, *Calvin on Common Grace*, p. 178.
16. *Institutes*, 2.2.12-17.
17. See J. Douma, *Algemene genade*, p. 19; S.J. Ridderbos, *De theologische cultuurbeschouwing van Abraham Kuyper* (1947); A.A. van Ruler, *Kuyper's idee eener christelijken cultuur* (1937); and C. Van Til, *Common Grace* (1947).
18. See the summary in G.M. Den Hartogh, "Dr. A. Kuyper's standpunt inzake de verhouding van staat en kerk," in *Antirevolutionaire Staatkunde* (January 1938), pp. 1-38.
19. *De Gemeene Gratie*, II, pp. 533-600.
20. See J.C. Rullmann, *Kuyper-Bibliographie*, III (1940), p. 255.
21. Van Ruler does not accept Christ's substitutionary atonement. See H.J. Langman, *Kuyper en de volkskerk* (1950), pp. 219ff, especially pp. 237-238.
22. K. Schilder, *Twee bijdragen tot de bespreking der "gemeene-gratie idee"* (Almanak F.Q.I., 1947); see also *Christus en de cultuur* (1947).
23. *Acta Synode Gereformeerde Kerken,* 1940-43, Article 682.
24. H. Beets, *The Christian Reformed Church* (1946), p. 108.
25. See D.H. Kromminga, *The Christian Reformed Tradition* (1943), pp. 145-146.

Chapter 14

1. *E Voto Dordraceno*, IV, p. 33.
2. *Gedenkboek* (1920), p. 35.
3. *Gedenkboek*, p. 85.
4. J.C. Rullmann, *Kuyper-Bibliographie*, III, pp. 261-264.

5. *De Heraut*, Sept. 24, 1905. For the J.H. De Vries translation, see *To Be Near Unto God,* p. 23.

6. Introduction to *Nabij God te zijn* (1908).

7. *Het sociale vraagstuk en de christelijke religie* (1891), p. 15.

8. *De Christus en de sociale nooden en democratische klippen* (1895), p. 45.

9. *E Voto Dordraceno*, I, p. 465.

10. *De Vleeschwording des Woords* (1887), pp. 10-11.

11. *Vleeschwording*, p. 87.

12. *Vleeschwording*, pp. 88ff; *Encyclopaedie der Heilige Godgeleerdheid*, II, pp. 160ff.

13. *E Voto Dordraceno*, IV, p. 535.

14. *Het werk van de Heilige Geest* (1888-89; English translation published in 1956 under the title *The Work of the Holy Spirit*).

15. *Pro Rege*, I (1911), pp. 468ff.

16. *Pro Rege*, I, p. 359.

17. *Pro Rege*, I, pp. 476-477.

18. *Pro Rege*, III, p. 212.

19. *Pro Rege*, III, p. 23.

20. *Pro Rege*, III, pp. 83-84.

21. *Pro Rege*, III, pp. 125ff.

22. *Calvinism*, second lecture.

23. *Pro Rege*, III, p. 132.

24. *Pro Rege*, III, pp. 184ff.

25. *Pro Rege*, III, p. 204.

26. *Pro Rege*, III, p. 447.

27. *Pro Rege*, III, p. 589.

Chapter 15

1. *De meiboom in de kap* (1913), p. 14.

2. P. Kasteel, *Abraham Kuyper*, p. 269.

3. D. Hans, *De man der kleine luyden* (1905), p. 27.

4. P.A. Diepenhorst, *Dr. A. Kuyper* (1931), p. 23.

5. Rullmann, *Kuyper-Bibliographie*, III, p. 347.

6. This phrase was coined by the Dutch historian Jan Romein in his *Erflaters van onze beschaving*.

7. Kasteel, *Abraham Kuyper*, p. 60.

8. See J.A. de Wilde and C. Smeenk, *Het volk ten baat* (1949), p. 249.

9. See *Het volk ten baat*, pp. 318-320; Rullmann, *Bibliography*, pp. 408, 434.

10. In his weekly paper *Hollandia*.

11. *De Meiboom in de kap*, pp. 21-22.

12. Rullmann, *Kuyper-Bibliographie*, III, p. 420.

13. *Om de oude wereldzee*, II, p. 239.

14. *Anti-Revolutionaire Staatkunde*, I, p. 544.

15. See A.B. David, *Een middeneeuwer in onze dagen* (1909) and J.L. Tal, *Jood en Jodendom in christen-omgeving* (1916).

16. Kasteel, *Abraham Kuyper*, p. 297; see also Kuyper's *Gemeene Gratie*, I, p. 387.

17. *Gedenkboek* (1921), p. 168.

18. *Wij Calvinisten* (1909), pp. 15-16.

19. *Anti-Revolutionaire Staatkunde*, I (1916), pp. 602-603.

20. Published in his *Forma ac Ratio*.

21. In *Geschiedenis der Christelijke Kerk in Nederland* (1869, edited by Ter Haar and Moll), p. 289; see also *Onze Eeredienst*, p. 39.

22. "The Antithesis Between Symbolism and Revelation" (a lecture delivered before the Historical Presbyterian Society in Philadelphia in 1899), p. 23.

23. *Onze Eeredienst*, p. 556.

24. In his review in *Ons Tijdschrift* (1911), pp. 761-781.

25. *Onze Eeredienst*, p. 30.

26. *Onze Eeredienst*, p. 47.

27. *Onze Eeredienst*, p. 85.

28. *Onze Eeredienst*, pp. 256-7.

29. See *Antirevolutionair ook in uw huisgezin; Ons program*, pp. 411-476; *Also gij in uw huis zit* (1899).

30. *Gedenkboek* (1921), pp. 79-80.

31. Article in *Onze Toekomst* (Chicago), issue of Nov. 19, 1920.

32. See the article by J. van Oversteeg, the secretary of the office of the Free University, in *De Rijpere Jeugd* of Dec. 15, 1920.

33. *Gedenkboek* (1897), pp. 155-156.

34. According to Prof. A.G. Honig, who was a student at the Free University at the time (see *De Bazuin,* November 12, 1920).

35. The complete letter is in Rullmann's biography, pp. 71-74.

36. In *Vir clarissimus F.L. Rutgers* (Student Almanac 1918).

37. "Bij de nagedachtenis van Willem Hovy," in *De Amsterdammer*, March 14, 1915.

38. *Gedenkboek* (1921), p. 16.

39. Kasteel, *Abraham Kuyper*, p. 8.

40. *Gedenkboek* (1897), p. 77.

41. A speech delivered on April 1, 1897.

42. See V. Hepp, *Herman Bavinck*, p. 163.

43. See J. Foret, *In Rapport met de Tijd* (1980), p. 114.

44. *Anti-Revolutionaire Staatkunde*, I, p. 485.

45. *Onze Eeredienst*, p. 179.

46. *Gedenkboek* (1921), p. 227.

47. *The Practice of Godliness* (1977 edition), pp. 65-66.

Chapter 16

1. As Kok himself told the journalist Brusse (*Nieuwe Rotterdamsche Courant*, February 5, 1927).

2. *Anti-Revolutionaire Staatkunde*, I, p. 559.

3. *Staatkunde*, I, pp. 568-569.

4. *Staatkunde*, I, pp. 116-119.

5. See *Staatkunde*, I, p. 424.

6. *Staatkunde*, II, pp. 535ff.

7. *Staatkunde*, I, pp. 265-266.

8. *Staatkunde*, I, pp. 418, 480.

9. In his sermon delivered on the last day of that year, in which he dealt with the theme "Repent, for the kingdom of heaven is at hand" (*Predikatiën*, 1913, pp. 374ff).

10. *Afgeperst* (1912), p. 65.

11. "Address to the Young People's Society in Kralingen," 1915 (Rullmann, *Kuyper-Bibliographie*, III, pp. 423-426).

12. Rullmann, *Kuyper-Bibliographie*, III, p. 465.

13. Frank Vanden Berg, *Abraham Kuyper* (1978), p. 263.

14. *Gedenkboek* (1921), pp. 15-16.

15. *Kasteel, Abraham Kuyper*, p. 83.

16. L.W.G. Scholten, "Kuyper als politicus," in *Gedenkboek* (1937), p. 235.

17. Kasteel, *Abraham Kuyper*, p. 337.

18. Among them were E.J. Potgieter (author of *Het Rijksmuseum* and *Jan, Jannetje en hun jongste kind*) and C. Busken Huet (author of *Het Land van Rembrandt*).